ENERGY OVER MIND!

*How to take control of your life
using the Mace Energy Method*

John Mace

'My finances, health, self-esteem
and general happiness have all
improved greatly.'

'Life is much more
enjoyable.'

'I lead a more positive and
productive life now.'

'I am also feeling very calm
within myself, whereas before
felt a lot of anger.'

'I am more centred and
loving than I have been
at any time.'

New York

"Not only will the Mace Energy Method put you on the path to emotional and   psychological health, it will also eliminate the stress underlying many physical health problems, leading to a marked improvement in your general health and well–being. The effects are astounding!

Having begun his working life as a mariner, John is an extraordinary man with an awesome intellect. In this book he explains in simple terms the scientific and philosophical concepts that underpin his work and takes readers on a journey of discovery as they follow these concepts through to their logical, and fascinating, conclusions.

The book "Energy over Mind" presents readers with an understanding of the mind that will leave even the most skeptical with the feeling that something has been explained to them that they ought to have known!

Used by trained practitioners around the world, the Mace Energy Method is a powerful tool for emotional healing that is having remarkable effects on peoples' lives. In a total departure from conventional counseling, it does not involve any self–disclosure and requires only one or two therapy sessions, which can even be carried out over the telephone.

In his compelling new book, John Mace describes the revolutionary concept of _Causism_ and its practical component, the Mace Energy Method, and explains how the unknowingly created negative identities that influence our lives and prevent us attaining our goals can be located and dis–created.

Based on years of research and study, this simple but extraordinarily effective therapy will allow you to regain control of your life and find the real you. Not only can it put you on the path to emotional and psychological health and eliminate the stress that underlines many physical health problems, it can also lead to a marked improvement in your general health, well being and confidence."

Jane Smith B.Sc (Honors)

Jane Smith worked for several years in medical publishing, first as an editor and then writing books for patients, before setting up her own company – Personal Heritage Publications (PHP) – to write and publish people's life stories for distribution amongst their own families and friends. PHP is still running successfully, but Jane now concentrates primarily on her work as a professional ghostwriter, writing books for commercial publication by some of the UK's top publishers.

Recently acclaimed by the editor at a major UK publishing company as 'the female Andrew Crofts', Jane has written many published books, including, most recently, the story of a young woman's struggle with body dysmorphic disorder – 'The Butterfly Girl' by Racheal Baughan, published in March 2008 by John Blake Publishing – and 'I Forgive You, Daddy' by Lizzie McGlynn, which is tipped to be another bestseller for Headline Publishing in 2009.

Energy Over Mind

How to Control Your Life Using the Mace Energy Method

ISBN 978-1-60037-607-8

Library of Congress Control Number: 2009923247

MORGAN · JAMES
THE ENTREPRENEURIAL PUBLISHER

Morgan James Publishing, LLC
1225 Franklin Ave., STE 325
Garden City, NY 11530-1693
Toll Free 800-485-4943
www.MorganJamesPublishing.com

In an effort to support local communities, raise awareness and funds, Morgan James Publishing donates one percent of all book sales for the life of each book to Habitat for Humanity. Get involved today, visit www.HelpHabitatForHumanity.org.

Contents

Preface   vii

Acknowledgements   xi

Foreword   xv

Introduction   xvii

Part 1   **Identities: the Basis of Causism
                and the Mace Energy Method**   **1**

Chapter 1   Identities: our alter egos   2
Chapter 2   Creating negative identities   36

Part 2   **Scientific and
                Philosophical Principles**   **53**

Chapter 3   The mind   54
Chapter 4   Time and the universes   90
Chapter 5   The real you   103
Chapter 6   Science, humanities and Causism   115

Part 3   **Applying the Mace Energy
                Method**   **125**

Chapter 7   Dis-creating negative identities   126
Chapter 8   Viewpoints   171
Chapter 9   Relationship repair   178
Chapter 10   How to realize your dreams   196

Part 4   **Where It All Began**   **209**

Chapter 11   My story   210
Appendix 1   References   237
Appendix 2   Testimonials   239
Appendix 3   Training and personal help   257

PREFACE

'I'm a born loser!'

'I can't get it out of my mind – I feel so guilty!'

'I'm not good enough!'

'Why do I keep doing that?'

'I wish I had his confidence.'

'If only they knew how I really feel!'

'That's how life is, and the sooner I accept it, the happier I will be.'

'I feel so useless!'

'Who really am I?'

Deep down within so many of us, amongst the clutter of negative thoughts and actions, these or similar thoughts lie festering. They persist for what seems like every moment of every waking hour of every day. If we do have a positive thought, a negative one quickly takes its place. The worst part is that we know there is nothing that can be done about it, because that is how we are; that's the hand that life has dealt us.

But the good news is that that is no longer true! Now something *can* be done about it, as many hundreds of people have already discovered. So why not you? The truth is that beneath all the negativity, the unhappiness, the frustrations and the apparent impossibility of realizing your dreams is the real you: the happy, positive and optimistic you. The unique information in this book, which is the result of a 50-year journey, demonstrates how the real you can be recovered. Within its pages are the secrets to life that have eluded every researcher since time immemorial.

Too good to be true, you think! Read on!

The importance of making my work more widely known was made evident a few years ago while I was watching a news item on television. The item concerned the aftermath of a notorious high-school shooting incident in America, in which many students and their assailants lost their lives. Understandably, those who survived suffered extreme trauma, which generated a host of trauma counselors to help them cope with their grief. There was a young girl on the programme who was so traumatized that she had to be assisted from the area, *after* leaving a counseling session.

This highlights the fundamental difference between the Mace Energy Method and conventional counseling:

clients may be in that state *before* they participate in the session, but not *after* it.

The television footage – which I watched when my own work was only partly developed – was a sadly dramatic example of a shortcoming of conventional counseling at work, no matter how well intentioned the counselor. Watching that unfortunate young woman being helped away confirmed to me just how effective the Mace Energy Method is in handling emotional problems.

With further research, the Mace Energy Method has advanced to such an extent that the gap between it and conventional counseling methods has widened beyond comparison.

Causism, the body of knowledge that underlies the Mace Energy Method, is an entirely new and revolutionary paradigm in emotional healing and, as with any revolutionary concept, it will have its skeptics. Every new idea spawns it's own equivalent of the 'Flat Earth Society', and one that challenges the theories and practices of Wundt, Freud, Jung et al. – in other words the very foundation of current psychology – is not going to escape controversy.

The Mace Energy Method raises an important and fundamental challenge to the need for narrative content and self-disclosure inherent in current methods of counseling. It has established beyond any doubt that there is no therapeutic benefit whatsoever in re-living or discussing emotionally distressing experiences and traumatic events. The only disclosure required is how a particular unwanted event affected the person emotionally, such as by making them feel angry, afraid, abandoned or lonely etc. – just single words, with no elaboration as to what occurred to make them feel that way. Very often, the relief expressed by clients when they realize that they do not have to re-visit some dreadful event that has occurred in their lives, such as a rape, is only equaled by their amazement that a process so seemingly simple can have such far-reaching positive effects.

Reading this book, you will gain an impression of the current me, not the old me who existed before my first psychic experiences. The old me was a pragmatic, materialistic individual with both feet planted firmly on the ground or, as one person reminded me, firmly on the deck in my days as a sea captain! I was ready to scoff at anything that could be called 'metaphysical'. Reincarnation? Give me a break! To say that my psychic experiences were instrumental in opening up a vastly broadened and distant horizon is a decided understatement. They opened up for me a vast panorama of life with limitless horizons and an intense interest in the spiritual component of the human race and its role in the pursuit of personal happiness and achievement.

John H.J. Mace
Perth, Australia

ACKNOWLEDGEMENTS

A special word of thanks is given to Jane Smith of Bristol, England. Her expertise and experience, plus her genuine interest in getting my work published, have turned my original manuscript into the book it is now. Her editing and advice deserve the highest praise and are sincerely and unstintingly given.

As for the work itself, to acknowledge all those who deserve a mention would be a formidable task, but sitting here contemplating the fact that some people must be acknowledged has turned my attention to Mr. Ron Knott, a teacher at the Palmyra Primary School, Western Australia, who did his best to make me believe in myself. He had more faith in me than I did in those distant years. I would like to think he is still around to read this, but, as unrealistic as that thought probably is, he deserves a mention nevertheless.

That my thinking has been molded by the writings of numerous philosophers and educators down the ages goes without saying, be they from ancient Greece, Asia or Europe, but from a practical point of view, Aristotle (384–322 BC), John Hobbes (1588–1679) and, more recently, Count Alfred Korzybski (1879–1950) deserve special mention.

Among the living who must be acknowledged is, first and foremost, my wife Pauline, who for many years has always been there by my side.

In the early research, John Avery was working in my Perth clinic with me. John is an old associate going back many years, and now runs his own Mace Energy Method clinic and training academy in New South Wales. His cooperation was invaluable, as were the encouragement and understanding of my sister Betty. It was my brother Eddie who, in the 1950s, pointed my nose in the direction of Korzybski and his understanding of time, and it was this act that totally changed my life.

Dr Mark Atkinson of London, with whom I shared my work, suggested the name Mace Method, with the comment 'Keep it simple.' Thank you, Mark. This has since been expanded to Mace Energy Method, thanks to a good friend Ron Campbell.

Another group, too numerous to single out individuals, is that of the clients who put their trust in me as the research continued. Perhaps, as events have unfolded, the expression 'guinea-pigs' would not be inappropriate as far as they are concerned, for without them I doubt that I would be penning this book. Theories and realisations are one thing, but 'the proof of the pudding is in the eating'! To them all I give my sincere thanks and gratitude for the trust they had in me.

FOREWORD

As a psychologist and counselor, I have long been aware that emotional trauma creates negative energy blocks in the body. But I have never found an effective procedure for 'de-creating' these blocks, until an extraordinary sequence of events led me to Murdoch University, where John Mace was lecturing on the theoretical principles of his revolutionary methodology.

This encounter not only led me to becoming a trained practitioner in this procedure, but it has also reinforced my belief that when you are ready to trust your intuition, people who have something important to teach you come into your life. I am so glad John came into mine.

John Mace has pursued his dream in his quest for knowledge, and in the process has developed and refined a dynamic procedure for locating and eliminating the emotional blocks associated with trauma. The concepts may initially appear revolutionary, but the process is so inclusive and interactive that the client cannot help feeling empowered by the procedure, which transforms notions of mind, body, spirit and identity into tangible realities. Tangible because the client participates at an experiential level in the process of identifying and eliminating unwanted identities using visual imagery. This unique method works rapidly and the outcomes are amazing and long term.

I am thankful for John's dedication to the task of perfecting the Mace Energy Method and am honored to be writing this Foreword.

Jocelyn Hardie

Registered Psychologist

BSc.Psych. Dip Counseling, Dip Ed.

INTRODUCTION

Since 1983, the author has resided in Fremantle, the port city in West Australia where he had his early formal education. One of six children, with a father away at sea more than he was at home, it was a matriarchal household, shared with maternal grandparents. The divergent personalities in a large working-class household provided an early introduction to the kaleidoscope of inter-personal relationships that feature prominently in this book.

It was from Fremantle in January 1943, at the age of 15, that John commenced his sea-going career as a junior deck hand. Whether he would have ventured to sea in days of peace is a moot point, but the turmoil of war saw his school commandeered by the army, and the resulting ad hoc school accommodation was the catalyst to his departure from school. With parental approval from a father who had himself run away to sea as a 14 year old, but with anguish from his mother, John joined his first ship.

When he first went off to sea he had no idea what a logarithm was and had never even heard of spherical trigonometry, which, before the advent of satellite navigation, were both essential in celestial navigation. By asking questions of those who knew and by delving into textbooks, he learned the art of self-education, and by the age of 27 was a fully qualified Master Mariner. He received his first command at the comparatively young age of 29, fully aware that the ability to read provides you with access to all extant knowledge – an awareness that proved invaluable in broadening his later research.

Being awarded command of his first ship at that early age resulted from an incident that occurred while John was serving as a chief officer. Just before sailing time one day, the captain, having consumed far too much alcohol, collapsed in his cabin, totally incapacitated, so John took it upon himself to take over. It seemed the logical and responsible thing to do for all concerned, both captain and company; so leaving the former in his cabin, he took the ship to sea. But news travels fast. With the ship back in its homeport of Hong Kong, he was ashore in the office when told to see the Managing Director, who, without even offering him a seat, said, 'I'm told you took her [the ship] to sea when you sailed.' The words were a blunt, matter-of-fact statement, which indicated that he was aware of the circumstances. Believing in the old saying 'least said soonest mended', John's response was a monosyllabic 'Yes.'

After a brief silence, the MD continued, 'Just like that! You just took over...and have not mentioned it. Were you going to report it?'

'No.'

'You are very fond of Jock [the captain] aren't you?'

'He has taught me a lot.'

Another brief pause and then 'Hmmm... I see' – and that was the end of that topic of conversation, brief and to the point.

Several days later, John was on a plane to take command of his first ship!

In his early years, John was affected by the claustrophobic ambience of his grandparents' Fundamental Christianity. Being unable to reconcile what he felt and thought with what he was expected to believe and practice, he rebelled – and shunned not only religion, but with it the spiritual side of life.

This attitude to spirituality changed dramatically in 1959, when a series of psychic experiences confirmed to him his true nature as a spiritual being. New insights concerning life and self caused him to shed the last vestige of religious dogma and ushered in a dramatic change in direction: he was on a new course in a search for the secrets of life. This change of direction coincided with shore-based employment as a harbor pilot, which enabled John to pursue his newfound interest.

He investigated many alternative therapies and modalities and trained as a counselor, but after 25 years of relying on the writings and research of others, he knew he hadn't found the answers he sought. The rainbow remained, but its pot of gold eluded him.

His spiritual experiences made it clear to him that the high aesthetic qualities such as happiness, enthusiasm, love and honesty are inherently normal in all sentient beings. Conversely, the myriad negative emotions such as depression, fear, loneliness, hate and self-doubts, which plague so many, are not normal. While emphasizing scientific explanations devoid of any religious connotations, the goal of his search became to find ways to allow people to realize and use their inherent potential as sentient beings.

The simplicity of spiritual awareness made John realize that if life itself is simple and uncomplicated, the real 'cures' for unhappiness must also be simple and uncomplicated. The common assumption and belief that life is complicated and requires complicated solutions has proven to be a fallacy. The year 1984 saw John forsake his maritime career, commence working as a counselor and begin a full-time search for the elusive answers to the questions of life.

Not having the 'benefit' of formal psychology training left John a free thinker in the fullest sense of the word – not hidebound by conventional ideas, religious or otherwise. His philosophy of learning parodies that of Descartes: 'I am! Therefore I can think and reason!' But despite all his reading and investigation of alternative modalities, the answers he sought were not there. The pot of gold was as elusive as ever.

However, John's freedom of thought eventually provided its reward, and after another 20-plus years, he found his pot of gold.

Although, as with any successful therapy, the practice of the Mace Energy Method has evolved over the years since John first began training students in 1998, the following extract from his original training manual still holds true today.

Causism is the name I have applied to a body of knowledge concerned with addressing and improving the human condition by a practical, or perhaps more scientific, look at the spiritual component of humankind. It is totally secular (non-religious).

'Spiritual' and 'secular' may seem a contradiction, but when you look at the schisms between various spiritual belief systems, such as Christians vs. Moslems vs. Hindus vs. Hebrews, and even within various religious groups, such as Christianity and Islam, you are forced to ask questions. For example, Catholics, Protestants and Jews all appeal to the same god, and there is incredible hatred and intolerance between the Sunnis and Shi-ites, but both appeal to Allah. Noting this, one cannot help but be driven to take a more scientific approach to the spirituality of humankind, devoid of any religious connotations, for it is obvious, to me at least, that all the religious overtones have corrupted the simplicity of the human

spirit.

If you are able to step back and figuratively separate the Physical Universe from the Spiritual Universe, you will note that all the great edifices of stone and masonry, no matter how grand and awe inspiring, all the colorful robes and paraphernalia, plus such practices as the burning of incense, are of the material universe, so that religion has become confused with materialism.

When viewing the incredible poverty in deeply religious countries in the so-called West, one cannot help but question current attitudes and beliefs. The answers certainly do not lie in the atheistic ideology of Communism, the materialism of the West, or among the numerous saffron-robed devotees of an Eastern religion that eschews worldly possessions as a road to spiritual enlightenment. Spiritual beings we may be, but we inhabit bodies and operate in the material world. Only by understanding this and finding a balance between the two will the answers be found, and with them true happiness. Knowing whom you really are is a basic requirement for true happiness, for that comes from within, not without. Causism is dedicated to this.

Causism is an evolving, empirical body of knowledge. Professional academy training takes this into account by creating two training levels, Basic and Advanced. The Basic Level is stable and the advanced level encompasses all changes. This book contains the Basic Level and all the revolutionary principles from which the Mace Energy Method has evolved. Anyone caring to use what is in this book can create amazingly beneficial life-changing effects on their fellows.

The advanced level contains additional research data, plus procedural refinements, none of which negates the fundamental truths upon which the Mace Energy Method is based.

Training and session details are in Appendix 3

Perth. January 2009.

No individual, no group, no organisation, no matter how big and powerful, has a lien on knowledge. Knowledge belongs to all.

PART 1

Identities: the Basis of Causism
and the Mace Energy Method

CHAPTER 1

Identities: our alter egos

All the world's a stage,
And all the men and women merely players;
They have their exits and their entrances;
And one man in his time has many parts...
[Jaques, As You Like It, William Shakespeare]

Some fundamental questions

Who am I? This is a question often pondered, but the infinitely more important question what *am I?* is seldom asked.

The answer to the latter is that you are a unit of human energy, the significance of which lies within the realms of science. Energy – including human energy – is indestructible, and therefore so are you; and if you are indestructible, you are also immortal. To answer the question *what am I? You are an indestructible, immortal unit of energy with infinite potential.*

But what about the question *who am I?* The answer to this is that you are a composite, comprising the *real you* plus all the parts you play in life, all your numerous *alter egos.*

The *real you* belongs in the high aesthetic zone where happiness, integrity, enthusiasm, serenity and a sense of well-being are inherently normal. Operating there, a person enjoys the good things in life and his or her dreams always materialize. Any aspects of life other than these natural attributes stem from negative identities, which are best likened to masks, the masks that hide the real you and that you unknowingly wear while acting on the stage of life.

Rudyard Kipling's poem *If* epitomizes aesthetic virtues.

If

If you can keep your head when all about you
Are losing theirs and blaming it on you,
If you can trust yourself when all men doubt you,
But make allowance for their doubting too;
If you can wait and not be tired by waiting,
Or being lied about, don't deal in lies,
Or being hated don't give way to hating,
And yet don't look too good, nor talk too wise:

If you can dream – and not make dreams your master;
If you can think – and not make thoughts your aim;

3

If you can meet with Triumph and Disaster
And treat those two impostors just the same;
If you can bear to hear the truth you've spoken
Twisted by knaves to make a trap for fools,
Or watch the things you gave your life to, broken,
And stoop and build 'em up with worn-out tools:

If you can make one heap of all your winnings
And risk it on one turn of pitch-and-toss,
And lose, and start again at your beginnings
And never breathe a word about your loss;
If you can force your heart and nerve and sinew
To serve your turn long after they are gone,
And so hold on when there is nothing in you
Except the Will, which says to them: 'Hold on!'

If you can talk with crowds and keep your virtue,
Or walk with kings – nor lose the common touch,
If neither foes nor loving friends can hurt you,
If all men count with you, but none too much;
If you can fill the unforgiving minute
With sixty seconds' worth of distance run,
Yours is the Earth and everything that's in it,
And – which is more – you'll be a Man, my son!

Rudyard Kipling (1865-1936). (Kipling, 1972, pp. 111–112)

One must, of course, look beyond the concept of gender in the last line, as it was actually addressed to Kipling's son.

The roles we play: our identities

We all play many parts and, just as the actors on a stage are immersed in their characterizations, obscuring their real persona, so too is our real self obscured by the roles we play in life, roles that are far too often not played by choice. While an actor is on the stage, all that the audience sees is the character that he or she is playing. The same applies to us all, for we are identified by the roles we are playing, and it is these roles that separate or distinguish us from others. Behind these roles lurks the real you, hidden by the masks you are wearing, for that is all the roles are – masks.

We call these masks *identities*, because you are identified by whatever mask you are wearing – by whatever role you are playing. Our identities are of two types: positive (pro-survival) and negative (non survival). *Positive identities* are knowingly created, whereas *negative identities* are unknowingly created during moments of *upset*.

The story of identities is rooted in the story of the alter ego, which is defined in *The Australian Oxford Dictionary* as 'A person's secondary or alternative personality', in *The World Book Dictionary* as 'Another aspect of a person's nature' and in *The American Heritage Dictionary* as 'another side of one's self; a second self'.

The American Heritage Dictionary also defines an identity as 'The collective aspect of the set of characteristics by which a thing is definitively recognizable or known' and 'the personality of an individual regarded as a persisting entity'.

Identities should not be confused with the concept of alter ego, which is a single entity: we are all impeded by numerous negative identities.

Every negative aspect of our lives – each negative thought, attitude and action that impedes our ultimate happiness and effectiveness – emanates from one of the negative identities that control us. The control these negative identities exert is real: the agoraphobic, who fears open spaces, is the product of a negative identity; an angry identity makes a person chronically angry; the person of low self-esteem is dramatizing or acting-out a low self-esteem identity; and all compulsive activity is caused by a hidden negative identity.

In a nutshell, everything one does not like about one's personality stems from a negative identity and, importantly, can be eliminated by using the techniques employed in the Mace Energy Method, described in this book.[1]

If any of the above strikes a chord with you and you feel the time has come to take some action to change things, read on, for you will find the means of achieving your dreams.

Identities, whether negative or positive, fall into three categories:

1. Our personalities,

2. Our activities,

---

1   The results for the many people who undergo sessions with trained practitioners are astounding. Although it isn't possible to practise the technique on yourself – for the reasons explained in Chapter 7 – the procedures are so inherently powerful that it is possible to achieve good results from a session conducted by a friend or someone else who, although not trained, has read the book and understands all the information it contains.

3. Our appearances.

It is the first two that are the subject of this book, but the third needs to be discussed in order to have a complete picture of the role of identities in our daily lives.

The concept of identities as separate, identifiable entities forming part of a person's make-up breaks new ground in understanding human nature. It is no longer *mind, body and spirit* (energy unit), but *mind, body, spirit* (energy) and *identities*. Identities are a fourth factor in the equation of life – the missing link in understanding human behavior – although if one were listing them in order of importance, *spirit* would come first.

The discovery of identities as separate entities has led to a quantum leap in the understanding of life and to the resolution of so many of life's previously insolvable vicissitudes.

The truth is that we cannot operate in life without identities. For example, spiritual beings (energy units) cannot drive motorcars, but an energy unit operating a body *may* be able to drive a motorcar, although not necessarily so: a 20-year-old person of normal intelligence with a healthy body does not necessarily have the ability to drive a car. There is a third, essential, ingredient required: *learning* how to drive a car, which is an identity – in this case, a *car driver's identity*.

THE FOURTH DIMENSION

To explain the concept further, identities are an absolute necessity for operating successfully in life. The driving-a-car scenario is used below to illustrate the concept in detail. If you do not know how to drive a car, substitute some other activity you have learned to perform quite competently – for example learning how to write as a child or learning how to type – and think back to the first time you started to learn it. Your own experience will be fundamentally no different from that of anyone else learning a new skill.

Gradually, with practice, they learn how to synchronize all the necessary actions to become a competent car driver. When they are familiar with all these actions, they drive without having to give much thought to the mechanics of driving, such as changing gear, which is dealt with automatically by their car driver's identity. They are then free to focus their attention on other things of more immediate interest – listening to music, talking to a companion or admiring the scenery – and to exercise the judgment required of a good driver, about speed and the car's path on the road etc. When people reach this stage, they delegate mundane driving activities to the identity that has been trained. If they did not create and train that identity, they would remain perpetual novices, driving would be a laborious and attention-consuming chore and they would be a menace on any high-speed motorway.

The same process applies to all activities involving training: sewing, typing, playing football or writing. *Training*, or *practice*, is an alternative term for *consolidating an identity*, so that the mechanics of the activity are handed over to the identity, leaving the person free to exercise judgment. This is a natural law of existence, and there are no exceptions.

All positive identities are created to solve the problems of day-to-day existence. A young woman feels her lifestyle is very limited by having to rely on public transport, so to solve the problems this creates she learns to drive – she creates a *car driver's identity*. A man finding that he has above-average natural skills in the game of golf adopts the identity of a professional golfer, and then relies on his golfing skills to survive financially. If he is having trouble putting, it means that his *golfing identity* needs correcting in the area of putting, so he starts practicing until his stance and grip come naturally and all his attention while on the green is on judging the putt.

Activity identities: developing personality traits

Every identity is created to solve some problem of our survival. If the young woman mentioned above did not think that learning to drive would enhance her lifestyle and make her life easier, she would not have bothered to learn to drive. This applies to every identity a person creates, and understanding it was instrumental in constructing this approach to personal development.

The following are examples of some of the *activity identities* of one man.

When he leaves for work and says 'Goodbye' to his children, he is in the identity of a *father*. At the front door, saying 'Goodbye' to his wife, he is in the identity of a *husband*. In his car, he assumes his *car driver's identity*. Once at work, he has a different identity again – his role as, for example, a *manager*. On his way home, he stops at the club for a few drinks and becomes *one of the boys*. Each and every identity has a different personality.

A decision to act always precedes the act itself, and as everything a person does requires an identity to carry it out, it follows that every decision a person makes requires an existing identity or the creation of a new one. If it is a new identity, it has to be practiced until the person is comfortable with it and can do the activity automatically.

The role of decisions in the creation of identities is of tremendous importance, as will be demonstrated later. Talking to the man in the example above at a football match would give you no idea as to what his occupation is, whether he is married or single, or whether he is a father. All you would be aware of would be his *football spectator's identity.*

Each identity has its own set of behavioral characteristics, which separate it from any other identity. Some of a person's identities do, of course, have similar traits, but each is unique in its own right.

It is a combination of dress and actions that usually gives the first noticeable or recognizable indications of a particular identity. But there are other aspects of this recognition that need to be understood in order to understand the ramifications of identities.

Your name is an identity: it is simply something by which *you* are known. *Your body* is an identity: it is something by which all your acquaintances recognize *you*. *Your occupation* is an identity: a person doing plumbing work is in the identity of a plumber. The words 'you' and 'your' are emphasized to establish that *you are an energy unit* and *not* one of your identities. You are separate from your identities; they are something that you own, something that you have created.

Personality traits superimpose themselves on all other identities. For every activity that a person engages in, a set of personality traits relevant to that activity is created and developed. As already stated, people can be categorized or recognized by three things – their outward appearance, their activities and, most importantly, their personalities. The individual's personality overarches the other categories, and is without doubt the overwhelmingly important aspect.

Take the example of a taxi driver: if you are in his taxi, his personality will predominate. Is he cheerful or grumpy, impatient or laid back and casual? Do what he perceives as other drivers' shortcomings stir him to anger, or does he just shake his head in amused tolerance? A taxi driver is in a *taxi driver's identity* the moment he commences to apply his trade; but along with that activity identity, there are any number of personalities apparent.

Another example of personality traits is the case of the man who leaves his family home in the morning and heads for work. As he is about to leave, he looks at the children, who are still having breakfast, and says quite sternly, 'Now do not forget! You two boys have to tidy up your rooms after school.' He walks to the front door, where he affectionately kisses his wife after saying; 'I'll get those concert tickets for our anniversary, and book a table at that restaurant your brother told us about.' In his car driving to work, he annoys the driver in front by blowing the horn because he is slow off the mark at a traffic light. On the motorway, he changes lanes about six times as he weaves through the traffic. When he arrives at work, he cheerily greets his secretary, thanks her for the report, which he read at home the evening before, and compliments her on her appearance: 'Those colors certainly suit you.'

We will leave him with his secretary and examine the various roles he has just played, for each role is an identity and each identity has its own recognizable personality traits.

As a *father* he is a stern disciplinarian, but if you asked him what his boys were wearing, it is doubtful that he would know. As a *husband* he is affectionate and considerate. *In the car* he is impatient and inclined to be a road hog. *In the office* he is cheery, observant and quick to praise.

Here we see four different identities, each with its own dominant traits or attributes – four different personalities all from the same individual. The man is dramatizing four different personality traits in four different situations, automatically adopting the identity appropriate to each. Further, each identity is a package of various traits, with the core trait predominating. Some personality traits are common in different identities, but no two identities contain an identical list of traits; there is always a variation to distinguish one identity from another. If, for example, shyness is a dominant trait in a person's make-up, it may be an element in several of

13

his or her identities. In this case it is known as a *chronic trait*, because it has multiple sources.

In the first example, the stern and authoritarian father is certainly demonstrating traits that are foreign to the man talking to his secretary, and both these traits are entirely foreign to the 'road hog' and to the caring, affectionate husband.

Outward appearances are not created in the same context as the personality traits, because people can change their outward appearance and their occupation by a self-determined decision. This is very important, and central to the concepts outlined in this book, because, unlike outward appearances, personality traits are fixed, good or bad.

We all have innumerable identities, and we all engage in numerous activities, each with its own collection of personality traits. It is the non-optimum personalities of individuals that this book is concerned with. For instance, being perpetually angry is hardly an optimum way to live, nor is being very shy, dishonest or overly critical of others, or any number of other similar traits.

The illustration on the following page (Johnson, 1998) illustrates three of the identities described above..

Illustration, EMMA GRIFITHS

Reproduced courtesy *The West Australian*.

Survival and self-interest

In his most famous work, *Leviathan*, first printed in 1651, the noted English philosopher Thomas Hobbes (1588–1679) contended that we are all motivated by self-interest (Hobbes, 1991). In translation, this means that our actions are linked to survival – our basic instinct. Survival dominates our existence. As *spiritual beings*, however, we cannot help but survive. No matter what happens to their bodies, beings survive. The primal urge to preserve one's life goes well beyond the mere preservation of the body. While this is, of course, a major factor, this urge really involves the preservation of every identity one has created, including the bodily identity.

In this context, to add substance to the survival concept underlying our activities, here is a paraphrased version of a discussion I had some time ago with a woman who disputed my contention that everything a person does, or decides to do, is purely a mechanism to aid, enhance or ensure survival. The conversation went something like this.

'Tell me something you have done that did not aid your survival?'

As quick as a flash she replied, 'I weeded my garden.'

'Okay. That must be a pro-survival action or you would not have done it.'

'You could hardly say that such a mundane thing as weeding the garden aided my survival.'

'I understand what you say, but who benefited from the weeding?'

'It was the garden that benefited, not me.'

'All right, but if weeding is such a chore, why do you have a garden?'

'You are not trying to make a fool of me are you?' she responded, and looked around at the others.

'No, no, no,' I assured her. 'I just want you to look at what is going on when you work in the garden. So why do you have a garden?'

'A house without a garden looks dreadful, as if no-one cares about it.'

'Okay. I take it that you feel happy when you admire your garden.'

'Of course! That's what a garden and gardening are all about. But weeding is still a mundane chore.'

'I understand that, but when you have finished

weeding and look back at your handiwork, how do you feel?'

'I feel quite good.'

'Obviously you feel better for having weeded the garden, so it is fair to say that the weeding has made you happier.'

'Ye e s.'

'Who would you say was surviving better – a person who laughs a lot and is happy, or a person who is sad and always seems unhappy about something?'

'The happy person of course.'

'Has happiness anything to do with survival?'

After a thoughtful pause, the smile on her face was answer enough.

I do not think there is any need to elaborate on *happiness* = *survival*, for the connection is obvious, although it could be put the other way around – namely, *survival* = *happiness*.

Pro-survival and non-survival decisions

Let us consider surviving through our identities, rather than only the survival of our bodies. To do this, take a hypothetical situation of a taxi driver who has lost his license through some infringement. The nature of the infringement does not matter, but being unable to continue as a taxi driver does matter. His *taxi driver's identity* is under threat! If he decides to appeal to the appropriate authority, what is behind that decision?

17

Being a taxi driver is an identity, and everything he subsequently does to re-instate his license is aimed at his survival as a taxi driver. He might argue that his very existence depends on his right to drive a taxi, but that is not really true, for there are ways of earning a living other than by driving a taxi. What he is actually doing is striving to maintain his identity as a taxi driver.

To obviate the argument that many of our decisions are non-survival because they worsen situations, it must be recognized that no decision has ever been made with the benefit of hindsight. No matter what the outcome of any decisions or actions, they were considered pro-survival at the moment they were made. Experience, of course, should create a tendency to make more correct decisions than incorrect decisions, but that does not alter the above statement. A decision always precedes an action, but remember that the pro-survival computation is always at the moment of decision. In the case of the woman weeding her garden, if a poisonous spider had bitten her while she was doing so, a new survival computation would have quickly taken over! Being bitten by a poisonous spider in no way negates the fact that the original decision to weed the garden was pro-survival. With hindsight, she would probably have put on some thick gloves, which would in itself have been a pro-survival action.

Can suicide be pro-survival?

One might argue that if everything we do is solely to

aid or enhance our survival, surely suicide must be an exception that invalidates this pro-survival concept. Indeed, this is a valid argument when one is only considering survival of the body, but the situation is not as simple as that. When people contemplate taking their own lives, it is because the pain they experience, whether emotional or physical, or both, is such that death would seem a better option. At the time of writing, the euthanasia debate rages in many Western countries, including my own country, Australia. Taking one's own life totally overrides any considerations about preserving the body. For the deeply religious person, death probably means surviving in heaven, and for those who believe in reincarnation it probably means survival in another body, both of which seem preferable to the current situation for those contemplating suicide.

Before proceeding further, I want to mention two relevant case histories of clients who were under the influence of identical *negative identities* – 'Life is not worth living!' I say their identities were negative – non-survival – because both clients had healthy bodies. They were both often despondent and depressed, one living in constant and unrelenting fear and on a daily diet of sedatives and tranquillizers going back many years. Both admitted to multiple suicide attempts, but did not have the 'courage' to see them through. Depression, fear, despondency and other unwanted feelings emanating from negative identities were the bane of their lives, with a consequent sense of the futility of living, despite good physical health and financial security. These two cases exemplify the fact that each and every negative identity acts in the same way: negative attitudes, thoughts and feelings pervade a person's life.

In light of the above suicide failures, another thing worth mentioning here is that it is probable that many people who have successfully committed suicide – for example by hanging themselves or jumping off a high structure – have found themselves unable to abort their attempts. An example of this from many years ago concerns a woman who attempted suicide by jumping off the Sydney Harbor Bridge. The chances of a person living to tell the story of such an episode are almost negligible, but she bucked all the odds and lived, although badly injured. (I can offer no details or references for this story, and am relying on memory from my days living in Sydney.) When well enough to relate her story, she said that as soon as she had jumped she wished she had not done so, but of course she was committed to her action and unable to abort it. One wonders how many of those people who have hanged themselves or have leapt to their deaths from a high structure have endured the same agonizing regrets when the survival instinct surfaced once they had taken the final steps in an irreversible act.

When discussing how suicide is pro-survival, two important elements need to be considered. First, if a person is experiencing suicidal tendencies, it suggests unhappiness – total apathy about life prospects. This also suggests that the person is in so much emotional and/or physical pain that anything is better than the life he or she is leading.

The second element concerns a person's innate sense of his or her own immortality as a sentient being. Remember, people are energy units and, as science will tell you, energy is indestructible – hence our immortality. Confirmed atheists aside – perhaps a very small minority of people – I have yet to meet anyone who refutes their own spirituality when it is pointed out that, from a scientific rather than a religious point of view, they are a spiritual being, an indestructible energy unit. Whether or not people are deeply religious, they have an innate knowledge of their own spiritual nature. In attempting suicide, they are likely to be thinking, 'This life is too unhappy, too traumatic,' or, 'This life is too painful … I will finish it off and start again.'

This concept is borne out both objectively and subjectively: objectively from my study and understanding of life in many of its facets, and subjectively from an out-of-body experience that occurred during a very troubled period of my life. (That experience, together with its circumstances, is related in the section entitled 'Death on a mountain' in Chapter 11.) On that occasion, finding myself detached from my body, and experiencing the calmness, serenity and euphoria of such a state, I had a very real sense that I was an immortal being, with the option of drifting off to start again with a new body in a different environment. It was only my sense of responsibility towards my young children that caused me to

21

return to my body. I can only say that as my life has subsequently turned out, it is probably one of the best decisions I have ever made, if not *the* best. However, when I considered the troubles of my personal life at the time, contemplating 'drifting off and starting again' was pro-survival for me at that moment. But from the perspective of that wonderfully illuminating factor hindsight, it was anything but pro-survival in the light of my subsequent life. Choosing not to 'drift off and start again' was no doubt a very pro-survival decision in the broader context of the well-being of my two children, and it was my own integrity as a father that surfaced to motivate the decision I made.

In my case, I was in the fortunate position of being able to change my mind, unlike some of those unfortunates who are unable to abort the action they have set in motion. It has to be emphasized that my decision was based on personal integrity and, although it may sound a little trite, the fact remains that personal integrity is our most precious possession, even above our own lives.

This fact will be very real to those who put their lives at risk when, for example, they attempt to save the life of another. It is what lies behind some incredible acts of bravery: people would not be able to live with themselves if they had not attempted to help.

Before we leave the subject of suicide, it is worth reiterating that it is intense physical and/or emotional pain that causes suicidal thoughts. Suicide due to intense physical pain for which medical science has no answer is beyond the scope of this book, but suicide due to emotional pain is not. Without a doubt, suicidal/depressive thoughts are the product of negative identities, which can easily be eliminated by anyone trained in the use of the Mace Energy Method.

The above considerations leave me in no doubt that thoughts of suicide, in the broader sense, are pro-survival for the individual concerned.

What about negative identities?

The concept of negative or non-survival identities sets up a paradox. If we create identities to aid our survival, how can we create negative identities that are non-survival? Some obvious questions accompany this paradox, for example:

- 'Why do we use these identities that do not enhance our survival?'
- 'Where do they come from?'
- 'Is it God punishing us?'
- 'Why do we not just change them if they adversely affect us?'

The most important question of all is probably:

- 'Why do we allow these identities to control us?'

These are the proverbial 64-million-dollar questions, which, I am very pleased to say, have been answered.

As stated above, the research I have been involved in now for many years has not only isolated negative identities, but has also provided the means to dis-create them, to free people from them, so that they regain control over their own lives. From this has come the mission statement: 'To assist people to be in control of their lives and live their own dreams.'

An important aspect of this paradox of creating non-survival identities is hindsight. As discussed earlier, hindsight is a very powerful weapon, wonderfully wise and almost infallible, but unobtainable until after the event! When given the opportunity to review the creation of their negative identities and to apply newly acquired hindsight, people always, without exception, nullify them. I speak not only from the objective reality that untold hundreds of clients have given me, but also from personal experience – subjective reality.

Responding and reacting: controlling your identities

Non-survival or negative identities operate against the wishes of the individual concerned. They are the source of obsessive–compulsive behavior, eating problems, irrational emotions, self-derogatory ideas, in fact anything that people feel is non-optimum in their personality and way of life. These are all activities or attitudes over which the person has lost control. Every one of them has its source in a negative identity, which is the driving force behind them, and it is the identity that dictates the behavior. The identity becomes stronger than the person who created it, and so the person is out of control.

The ideal tyranny is that which is ignorantly self

administered by its victims. The most perfect slaves are therefore those which blissfully and unawaredly (sic) enslave themselves. *(Dresden James quotes)*

Put another way: The ideal tyranny is the negative identity that has been unknowingly created and that then proceeds to control and 'unawaredly' enslave the individual who created it.

How often have you heard someone say, 'Gees, he makes me angry!' Actually, there is nothing further from the truth than that statement.

One person says or does something and a second person reacts to it by becoming angry, yet a third person in the same situation just laughs, thumbs his nose or, showing total disdain, turns and walks away. This third person was not reacting, he was responding, which highlights the vast difference in attitudes. To respond is rational and pro-survival for the individual, but to react is irrational and non-survival for all concerned.

The cause of the vast difference between reacting and responding to some outside effect is found in the negative identities. What is being looked at here is the nature of the personalities of the second and third people. Whatever they experience is their own creation, stemming from their own personalities, their own identities. It appears that what was done or said by the first person caused anger in the second, but the reality is that the real reason for the anger lies within the personality of the second person. Something within his own personality was triggered and he reacted with anger, but the anger and any other feelings he

25

experienced were entirely of his own creation – a negative identity in full cry.

This discussion takes no account of what was said or done, for no matter how gross or uncalled for in the eyes of the second person, or whether his reaction was justified, it does not alter the fact that he created his reaction to it – under the influence of a negative identity.

Feelings and emotions are totally subjective. No one has a hypodermic syringe full of emotions or feelings, pleasant or unpleasant, with which to inject others. Therefore every emotion a person experiences is self-created, and it follows that he or she is the only one who can dis-create it.

If you look at it logically, anger very seldom helps any situation. In fact, situations are invariably worsened by it, for an angry person is, to a degree, out of control, and says or does things that are often regretted, particularly with respect to the rather brutal maxim, 'You are ultimately responsible for everything that you experience.'

There is, however, a positive side to this. If people are totally responsible for creating their own feelings, they are also capable of eliminating any unwanted feelings and, in fact, have a responsibility for dis-creating them – provided they know how to do so.

Before continuing, it is worth examining the effects of these negative (or non-survival) identities further in order to put the underlying research into its proper perspective.

A tragic example can be seen in the organisation known as Alcoholics Anonymous (AA). I want to make it clear that I am not opposed to the help this organisation affords its members; it is responsible for many people being able to lead healthy and productive lives. The tragedy as far as I am concerned is the belief that alcoholism is a bodily disease. Members stand up and say, 'I am an alcoholic,' but there is nothing further from the truth. They are not alcoholics; 'they' are sentient beings that have an identity addicted to alcohol. I have helped too many people overcome their addiction to alcohol to think otherwise. The interesting thing is that once individuals have rid themselves of the relevant identities, they are free to drink alcohol if they wish, for they are now in control of their lives. They do not necessarily have to become teetotal, a total abstainer (few do), because consuming alcohol is an everyday event for many people, especially in social situations.

An example of a negative identity in action is a woman who has just been accused of physically abusing her children, much to the amazement of her work colleagues: 'But Jean is so easy-going and considerate. She wouldn't hurt a fly!' In her at-work identity she obviously would not hurt a fly, but in her mother identity she obviously hurts more than flies! Two different identities are dramatizing two vastly different personalities in the same person. It is the presence of identities that explains the sometimes diverse and conflicting behavior manifested by individuals at different times.

27

Here is a real-life example. Several years ago, I knew a couple who had lived perfectly happily together for quite a few years and who had two young children by the time they decided to get married. They married because it was made clear to them that their de-facto relationship was incompatible with the creed of the religious group they had joined. Within three months of formalizing their relationship they were in the divorce court, and subsequently parted on not very amicable terms. So what happened? At the time, I was not the only observer to be perplexed, but my research into the role of identities has now given me an answer. Their respective pre-marital identities were perfectly compatible, but his husband identity and her wife identity were anything but compatible, for very different personality traits quickly emerged – hence the divorce.

There is a natural law of the universe that is carved in granite: a person will never knowingly create a negative identity. This law is accompanied by another: *You are only affected by what you are unaware of.* The natural urge to survive is so overwhelmingly powerful that when people locate a hidden negative identity and neutralize it, because they now know all about it and how it has affected them, they will never create it again.

The answer to all the questions people have about their shortcomings lies in the negative non-survival identities – identities that have all been unknowingly created. To introduce an optimistic tone to this writing, the method that has been researched and developed addresses and eliminates these negative identities, and in doing so puts people on a road that leads them to eventual control of their own lives.

The programme in us all that activates the creation of identities is an automatic response, triggered by the primal urge of survival. It goes into action as a stimulus–response mechanism. But there are invariably two sides to every coin and, in the grand scheme of things, the possibility that the programme that automatically creates survival identities would also, of its own accord, create negative non-survival identities was apparently not considered. It is the old hindsight situation again: at the moment of its creation, the identity appeared to aid the person's survival, but it does not do so in the longer term. The ultimate answer to this enigma lies in the difference between a person and a spiritual being or energy unit.

As to the question 'Why do we allow these identities to control us?' the answer is that the being unknowingly gives them too much power, more power than the being itself retains in that particular activity. Fortunately, the identity has no inherent power of its own, which is why it can be eliminated. An analogy is readily available in a car battery. A battery stores energy but does not create it. It is entirely dependent on the car's charging unit for all its energy, all its power. Disconnect the battery and it soon goes flat – the lights do not work and, more importantly, neither does the self-starter. With all its power gone, the battery is lifeless and useless. This is basically what the developed procedure does: it symbolically disconnects the identity from the being and then drains off the identity's energy so that it is unable to function. The identity then becomes lifeless, allowing the person to take control in that area of life.

A prerequisite to the elimination of a negative identity is, of course, that the person is made aware of its existence.

The question may now arise as to why the being gives the identity any energy in the first place. The answer is that energy is an essential element in any action – no energy, no action. Go back to the car-driving identity. If a person wants an identity to assume responsibility – the mundane mechanical aspects of shifting gears etc. – while he or she concentrates on safety aspects, the identity must be given energy to do it. This may sound a strange concept, but if you carefully examine it, the truth will be apparent. Nothing can operate without an energy source, but the only power any identity has is what it receives from the being that created it. The being has to supply the energy for the identity to keep operating. Although the identity is energy, just as a being is energy, the difference lies in the fact that the being is a natural source of energy whereas the identity is not.

The identity gaining more power than its creator is best likened to a ball of snow: it may start off as no bigger than your hand, but if you roll it in the snow, it continues to grow bigger and will eventually become so big that you cannot move it – you do not have enough power to overcome its inertia. Exactly the same applies to any identity: the more you use it, the stronger it becomes. People train in, or practice, an activity to hone the skills they need to carry it out. What they are really doing is strengthening the identity that has to carry out those skills – the more the identity is used, the stronger it becomes.

If that is the case, why doesn't the being simply remain as the overt energy source for the activity, instead of delegating it to the identity? If that happened, we would be back to square one, having to continue to concentrate our attention on the activity, and thus negating the purpose of having the identity in the first place.

Practice makes perfect

Even identities knowingly created for playing sport can develop faults, hence the need for a coach to point this out to the sportsman or sportswoman, who must focus on overcoming the developed fault. Overcoming the fault is achieved by practicing the remedial actions until the old action is overridden and replaced by the new one. A golfer who modified his or her stance while putting would ultimately adopt the new stance without having to think about it – thus creating a new *golfing identity*.

Pro-survival identities are knowingly created, unlike negative identities. When people have knowingly created an identity, they can knowingly change it. In the case of a *golfing identity*, because someone has knowingly created it, he or she is ultimately in control

31

of it and can modify it at will. The person can play golf or not play golf; it is their decision – unlike an addict, who is controlled by identities.

If a person can modify a knowingly created activity and, even in the example of golfing, simply cease the activity, why is it not possible to do the same with aspects he or she does not like? The answer is that the person has first to be aware of the existence of the aspect to be able to do anything about it. The golfer was overriding the identity aspects that he or she did not like because they were non-survival as far as golf was concerned.

The key words here are *knowing* and *knowingly created*. Unwanted behavior is that which is out of control because the identity that manifests it was *not knowingly created*. If there is something that people do not like about themselves, it emanates from an identity over which they have no control – if they did have control, they would simply change it.

Spiritual beings as energy units

Each negative feeling that people experience is so deeply ingrained that they assume it embodies *who* they are. But it does not: it is a negative identity. More insidious is the fact that negative identities dictating attitudes are always acted out in life. It is not that the person has a voice in his or her head saying, for example, 'I am inferior.' Rather, it is a sense of inferiority pervading that person from negative identities. This highlights the fundamental truth that *identities are not you; they are something that you have unknowingly acquired.* Even if people *know* from a rational point of view that they are not inferior, if they are the victims of such a negative identity, it moulds their personality and dictates how they behave in life. For no matter how irrational from a logical and objective viewpoint, that is how they see themselves and how they live their lives.

One of my clients located two identities: one had always made her feel *useless*, and the other made her feel *frustrated*. Such a case is referred to as the person's *ruin*: it was the bane of her life. It took just 20 minutes to dis-create the identities, to banish them from her life and from her universe.

Every conceivable negative consideration that people can have regarding themselves can be eliminated, for it is not the person but a negative identity generating the feeling.

Let us use *feeling powerless* as another example, and let me state that this particular example is not a figment of my imagination. I have lost count of the number of clients who have uncovered that very same self-derogatory idea: all their lives they have felt powerless. Here we have the 'chicken and egg' syndrome in full display. What came first? Did the failures in life generate the feeling of being powerless, or did the identity generate the powerless feeling that caused the failures? Whatever came first, once that identity is in place, unless it is eliminated, the individual concerned will experience the feeling of powerlessness for the rest of his or her life.

Below is a testimonial from someone who was plagued by an obsessive compulsion to keep cleaning her house. It illustrates that all unwanted behavior is an out-of-control, unwanted, negative identity that takes over a person's life. Compulsive behavior is an overt example of insidious negative identities that are not only self-deprecating but also easily recognized by the activities they manifest. These identities control people's attitudes to themselves and to others.

> Although I have done many years of therapy, I felt I needed to come to you for I had a few unhandled [sic] issues to clear. I was a compulsive house cleaner; spending much of my waking time wasted 'keeping busy'. Since the session, all compulsion to clean my house has gone. I also worked with you on an issue of shame, which I now find I can openly express instead of hide. I am also feeling very calm within myself, whereas before felt a lot of anger. Your work seems so easy, but definitely worked for me.
> Thank you.
> Pauline

This is an interesting case. Pauline came for help on her mother's advice to address the irrational guilt she felt because of some silly mistake she had made in her teens. As expected, she went away totally free of that irrational feeling. A week later, her mother informed me that since the session Pauline had ceased her compulsive house cleaning and had adopted a normal house-cleaning routine. I had had no idea that she was a compulsive house cleaner, and it was never mentioned during the session. But what happened is a testament to the efficacy of the procedures in ridding people of compulsive behavior, irrespective of what it is. Pauline came to the session plagued with an irrational feeling of guilt; she had no idea that it was connected to her compulsion.

This demonstrates the point that people are only the effect of what they do not know about. The fact that Pauline's session only lasted for approximately an hour testifies to the power of the modality. In that short space of time she had totally dealt with 18 years of compulsive behavior that had not responded to any other treatment.

Chapter 2

Creating negative identities

Upsets

To understand how and why a negative identity is created, it is necessary to understand the meaning of an *upset*. In general usage, it is an emotional disturbance. Further, however, an upset is *anything that a person does not experience by choice*. No one ever willingly experiences anything that is emotionally disturbing. The importance of this definition lies in obviating the need to classify upsetting experiences. No matter what has been experienced, if it is unwanted, it is an upset, and many experiences fall into that category. At one end of the spectrum of upsets are, for example, rape, extreme physical abuse, devastating accidents and violent arguments. At the other end are disappointments, bad news and losses – both emotional and material. The important consideration in these examples is: was it wanted? The Mace Energy Method is only concerned with how someone was emotionally affected and how he or she reacted. The circumstances of the upset – when it happened, why it happened, who was involved, what happened and how long it lasted – are totally irrelevant. This is a total departure from conventional counseling.

Let us now revisit the nature of a spiritual being, an energy unit, so named because that is all it is – energy, purely and simply. All sources of energy radiate energy: the sun radiates heat and light; an electric heating device is known as a radiator because it radiates heat, as well as a little light; an electric light bulb radiates mainly light, as well as some heat. The psyche is energy, and as such it radiates energy commonly referred to as *flows* or, colloquially, *vibes* – hence the expression, 'She has beautiful flows; she is a lovely person to be with,' or the reverse, 'He has terrible vibes; I cannot stand him!'

The unwanted feelings that always accompany an upset are automatically resisted – and *what is resisted persists*. It is these feelings, not the event itself, that are addressed in the Mace Energy Method. In the case of physical abuse, a person may be able to fend off the attacker, but the event has already exerted its emotional impact, and it is this that needs to be dealt with, for it is the emotional effect that lingers. In this scenario, adverse energy impinges on the person, who resists the incoming vibes with his or her own energy in a natural attempt to ward off what is being experienced. Now we have two opposing forces –

science's immovable object and its irresistible force. The only outcome can be the development of a *ridge* between them. In the physical world there is a simile: the Himalayan mountains were formed by two of the Earth's plates moving against one another, resulting in the welling up of a great mountainous landmass. The mountains contain all the landmass that was directly involved in the collision. In the case of an upset, there is a ridge of negative energy, and locked into that *energy ridge* are all the unpleasant emotions and negative aspects experienced in the upset, every single one of them.

Energy ridges

Energy is invisible, so the energy ridge is also invisible, but the effect created certainly makes its presence felt – the presence of energy is only recognized, or made known, by the effects it creates. Again, very importantly, *what is resisted persists*, so the energy ridge stays in place no matter where people go; they take it with them, even if they go to another country. This is why some people still complain about something that happened to them 20 years ago: they are still feeling the effects of the energy ridge created during the upset, which they are carrying around with them, as it clings like a magnet no matter where they go.

The mechanics of *what you resist persists* are interesting – and are fundamental to the Mace Energy Method. Whenever you think of something, your mind creates a mental image of it. If someone says,

'Resist looking at it!' the obvious rejoinder is, 'Resist looking at what?' As you do not know what it is you have to resist picturing, you have formed no picture, no mental image. But if the person then says, 'I want you to resist picturing a cat,' you immediately create an image of a cat. So this exercise traps you into picturing a cat as long as you resist it. The image of the cat will only disappear when you cease resisting it, and focus your attention on something else. On the other hand, by repeatedly saying, 'Resist looking at a cat. Resist looking at a cat. Resist looking at a cat,' you will be trapped into the continuous creation of a picture of a cat.

It is this *continuous creation* syndrome that is behind the continuous creation of the energy ridge and all its negativities. Exactly the same syndrome occurs when people resist unpleasant emotions from an upset – they continually create them.

A trauma is a painful experience, either emotionally or physically. Herein we are concerned with emotional trauma, emotionally painful experiences – upsets. Pain of any kind, whether it is emotional or physical, lowers a person's awareness. Overwhelming pain produces total unawareness, which is unconsciousness. There are degrees of pain, from slight discomfort to the overwhelming pain that causes unconsciousness, and there are degrees of unawareness, depending on the pain.

An example of unawareness is provided by an incident in which a man hurts his leg and feels intense pain. He will probably grab hold of the injured part and hobble about, if he can. While hobbling about, he will not be very aware of what is going on around him, as all his attention will be on the pain in his leg. His awareness has been lowered, and he would be hard pressed to recall later what was happening around him. After a physical injury, there is often no recall of the event, and the period of time covered by the loss of memory will be governed by the severity of the pain, and will extend to include periods before and after the experience.

Exactly the same reaction occurs with emotional pain: awareness is lowered and the memory of what happened is reduced.

In an upset, there may be no physical pain, and whether there is or not is of no importance, for there is always emotional pain. A sentient being automatically avoids pain because it is non-survival. Just as we keep our bodies away from the danger of intense heat, so too will we avoid emotional pain – by keeping our attention away from it. We occlude it, and that occlusion is a natural pro-survival phenomenon.

I can recall as a young lad finding myself in the middle of the road with my bicycle lying nearby. I was not really hurt, but I had no memory of how the accident happened, only of being a couple of hundred yards back up the road from where I picked myself up afterwards. My physical injury was very minor, and what appears to have caused the brief memory loss was the emotional impact of the accident. But I only discovered the emotional aspect when I examined the incident many years later and recovered the memory of what had happened.

Learning the art of acceptance

In emotional trauma, the energy ridge is of the person's own making. This may seem a harsh statement, but the brutal truth is that if he or she had not resisted the incoming vibes of the upset, there would be no ridge of energy. 'Turn the other cheek', a saying from the Christian Bible, comes to mind. The implication is: 'do not resist what is happening! Let the emotional effects flow past you.' As a friend once said to me, 'If you can accept what is [the situation], the world is your oyster.' Rudyard Kipling espoused this viewpoint in his beautiful poem *If*. It is the act of accepting what has happened that flows through the poem.

The two keywords here are *responding* and *reacting*. Responding is rational, but reacting is irrational, and this is the message so eloquently portrayed in the poem, particularly with the lines:

Or watch the things you gave your life to, broken,
and stoop and build 'em up with worn-out tools:
If you can make one heap of all your winnings

And risk it on one turn of pitch-and-toss,
and lose, and start again at your beginnings
and never breathe a word about your loss...

(Kipling, 1972, p. 112)

These lines illustrate a person's acceptance of the

situation for what it is, and then just getting on with life without reacting with blame, regret or 'what if...'

In Japanese folklore, the bamboo is compared with the sturdy oak. In a gale, the oak tree resists the wind and is often damaged, even torn up by its roots, whereas the bamboo doesn't resist it: it bends and then stands erect when the gale has passed.

If people do not resist what is happening and bend to the wind, so to speak, they are more likely to go through life serenely, without bickering and criticizing others, accepting what life dishes out, but at the same time not bowing to circumstances, descending into apathy, or making irrational decisions. They may not agree with what they see, but they will *respond* rationally and not become the effect of it.

I can assure you that this is not some Utopian dream; such high states of life and living are attainable. Remember that *adverse reactions* go hand in hand with *negative identities*. Rid yourself of your negative identities, and your dreams *will* come true.

To return to the concept of accepting 'what is', here is a useful analogy. If a man walks up to his car and sees that a tire is flat, that is how it is. No matter what his reaction, the fact is that the tire is flat, and in *that moment* of time it will never change. He can wave a magic wand and inflate the tire, but that is in the future; in the present moment, the tire is flat. Railing about the situation, for example how it came about, how unlucky he was etc., will not change anything. The only thing that is subject to change is what he does about it: accepting that it is flat, and doing something rational about it. Doing that 'something', however, is in the future, not now. A person cannot change what has happened, so the sooner action is taken, the sooner the focus is on the future.

This concept applies to handling people's negative identities and explains why, with the Mace Energy Method, there is no interest in either what happened during an upset or why it happened. The least helpful thing to do is to ask why. *Why* is totally irrelevant. The only reason to ponder why, after you have handled the situation, is to learn from it, and to prevent a re-occurrence.

Upset phenomena

Having accepted that negative identities are unknowingly created, it remains to explain the circumstances surrounding their creation. To summarize: all negative identities are associated with upsets during which a person's awareness is lowered.

Drawing A in the diagram on page 45 represents a person who is happy and out-flowing. Drawing B shows some of the mechanics of an upset, for example the result of a disappointment. It illustrates the person becoming 'down in the mouth', with their attention on themselves, because the upset has lowered their mood.

The arrow going from right to left represents the initial unwanted feeling of the upset. The additional

43

arrow represents the energy exerted by the person to resist the unwanted feelings – where the arrows collide is a ridge of negative energy.

The illustrations are purely graphical. For example an unwanted vibe or feeling does not come from an external source – the event is external, but the vibes emanate from within. *Anything you feel is your own creation.*

To demonstrate this, when people are upset by some thought, it is not necessarily pertinent to the current environment, for they may have been daydreaming about some long past event that upset them.

UPSET PHENOMENA

A

HAPPY & OUTFLOWING

B

NEGATIVE ENERGY RIDGE

RESISTANCE TO FEELING

UNWANTED FEELING

LOW MOOD & INTERIORISED

UPSET PHENOMENA

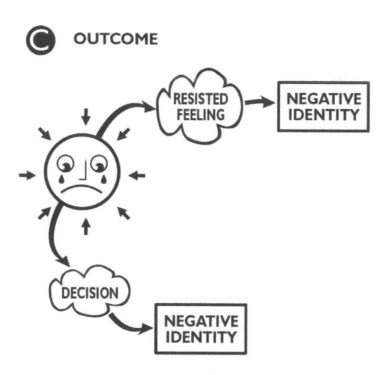

The graphic nature of the illustrations unavoidably shows the energy ridge forming away from the body, but this is not necessarily the case, for it can form anywhere, on, around or within the body. The person always feels the impact of the energy ridge, no matter where it is centered.

When someone is upset, their mood level inevitably drops, because they feel under threat to some degree. If they did not feel threatened by the event, they would not have resisted the experience, and there would have been no upset in the first place. The lowered mood level is a salient link in what subsequently happens, for a person who is at a low mood level does not make positive decisions. An angry person has yet to make a positive pro-survival decision, but more of that later.

The arrow to the right in the first diagram is labeled *Unwanted Feeling*, for the initial feeling that the person resists forms the ridge. There are always other unpleasant emotions and feelings locked in the ridge, but it is the *initially resisted feeling* that is of paramount importance. It is this feeling that overwhelmed the person and caused the upset. As it is unpleasant, the overwhelming feeling is resisted, and because of this resistance, it persists, unknowingly buried in the psyche to become a negative identity.

The survival urge

At this point, another factor, the *survival urge*, emerges. As mentioned in Chapter 1, our personal survival is Paramount, with a capital P. It is more than 350 years since Thomas Hobbes published his book *Leviathan*, in which he expounded the fundamental of all urges – *survival* (although he referred to is as *self-interest*). The more one examines the simplicity, subtleness and enormous importance of this urge, the more ironical it seems that it has taken more than 350 years for someone such as myself to reap the full benefits of Hobbes' work, for this paramount urge is central to much of the developed procedures of the Mace Energy Method. In some circles, the concept has been, and maybe still is, viewed in the derogatory self-interest sense, but if you ask yourself who the most important person is, a genuinely honest answer will be 'Me!' It is not without reason that Hobbes is recognized as one of the greatest English-born philosophers.

As survival is our primal urge, we are continually making survival decisions to cope with events that threaten us. If we feel hungry, our survival urge makes it a normal reaction to decide to eat: if we do not feed our bodies, ultimately they die. If we are thirsty, we decide to drink. If we are walking down the road to a bus stop to go somewhere important and the bus we want to catch comes around the corner, we will probably decide to run so that we do not miss it. There is nothing dramatic and earth shattering about these mundane events, but they demonstrate that the survival urge is not only paramount and continuous, but automatically stimulates a continuous stream of appropriate pro-survival decisions.

Similar responses occur with an upset, but the person making a decision to handle the perceived threat does so from an unfortunate position. They are down in the mouth; their mood level has dropped into the negative survival band, which draws forth an anti-survival, negative computation. The mood of the decision always matches the mood level of the individual at the time. For example, a happy person has happy thoughts, an angry person has angry thoughts, and an optimistic person has optimistic thoughts.

Similarly, decisions mirror the mood of the person.

A reduced awareness level, occluding the decision and its emotional pain, compounds the error in decision-making, and as soon as the decision is made, it becomes buried in the psyche, to sit there like a hypnotic command. A recent case history gives an example. To accompany 'frustration', a lady decided 'I am useless!' She had metaphorically 'shot herself in the foot', and this derogatory attitude permeated her life.

A decision is depicted below the face in drawing C in the upset phenomena diagram on page 46. This decision becomes embedded in the psyche, definitely out of sight, but not forgotten. It becomes another negative identity, acting like a hypnotic command, needing to be lived out on cue.

To explain the diagrams in detail, when someone is upset, a rapid series of events occurs. First, the person resists the overwhelming negative or unpleasant feeling, so that the dictum *what you resist persists* comes into effect. When we resist any unwanted, unpleasant feeling, its subsequent persistence consolidates it, and entrenches it as part of our make-up, part of our personality. This is because the upset was, of course, emotionally painful, therefore the being occludes it from memory, from conscious recall, and having forgotten that we resisted it, we are also unaware that it is persisting below conscious awareness level. We have unconsciously created a *negative identity*. For example, if someone was overwhelmed by a sense of inferiority, that is going to become the story of that person's life. Whatever they achieve in life, no matter what status they may enjoy through their endeavors, they are blighted by a sense of inferiority. Just as in the analogy of a ball of snow being rolled along in the snow, the identity grows bigger and more powerful through use, and gathers other negative traits until it dominates the person who created it.

Every negative identity is a package of numerous negative traits. Notes from one of my sessions list negative traits ranging through unwanted emotions of *anger, hopelessness, frustration, self-pity* and *self-judgment*. All these traits formed a negative aspect of the person's personality.

To digress for a moment from this self-derogatory decision-making, Einstein contended that we only use 10% of our abilities, and Jung is credited with going even further by saying we only use 1%. But it is not that we only use small amounts of our potential; we use it all, but *against* ourselves in the form of negative identities. Every decision made as a result of an upset is similarly derogatory. Take the case of the woman previously mentioned who was plagued with feelings of uselessness. During an upset, she had reacted with the observation, or decision, 'I am useless.' She was not useless, but she had created a negative identity that permeated her personality, stimulating an insidious feeling of being useless no matter what she achieved. The logical questions to arise from this are: 'why should a person make such a self-deprecating decision about themselves? Why not make it about someone or something else?' The answers are as logical as the questions when the circumstances are explained.

In drawing B in the 'Upset phenomena' diagram, as an immediate result of the upset, the person focuses all their attention on themselves. In consequence, their awareness of their immediate environment is greatly reduced or, in some cases, depending on the pain and trauma, is totally non-existent. This is an automatic response whenever a person is in physical or emotional pain because the survival urge compels them to focus their attention on themselves. If one is thinking about football, one is not going to make decisions about Aunt Martha, horse racing or tonight's movie. Similarly, if one's attention is on oneself, any decision will be about oneself, and not about something extraneous.

> In combination, self-attention and low mood levels produce non-survival decisions about self.

It is important to understand that all this happens within a split second of the initial impact of the upset, so any decision is not made with the luxury of hindsight or with the benefit of even a moment's reflection. It is only in the aftermath that people deflect some attention from themselves, become aware of their immediate surroundings, and thus make decisions directed at their immediate environment, such as figuratively lashing out at someone or something. This is very common in bouts of anger. The speed and degree to which it happens are governed by many factors, for example by the person's chronic mood level and the severity of the pain and anguish of the upset. Although the person may subsequently start looking outward at their environment, the personal damage to their self-esteem has already occurred – the non-survival decision sits there and acts like a hypnotic command, being dramatized or acted-out thereafter. This is the source of every self-derogatory feeling people have about themselves, every feeling of inferiority and low self-esteem, from a nagging sense of worthlessness to the simple 'I am not good enough.'

PART 2

Scientific and Philosophical Principles

CHAPTER 3

The mind

My brethren we can no more think about anything without a mental image appearing than we can live without breathing. (Nikhilananda, 1987, p. 214)

Socrates is credited with saying, 'Understanding begins with the definition of terms.' To have any understanding of the mind, we need to be more knowledgeable about what it is. Therefore I will stick my neck out here and state that I am probably the first person in recorded history to actually define the mind, to state what it is and what it does. My definition is as follows.

The mind is an abstract and intangible entity whose only function is to create a mental image of what the person has their attention on. It has no weight, size, color or form.

It should be noted that because the mind is totally abstract and intangible, it couldn't be defined in materialistic terms, so that its function is an essential component of its definition. To elaborate on that definition:

> The mind does not store knowledge, create emotions, rationalize or make decisions. Every function ever attributed to the mind is actually the province of the being, so that everything previously written, taught, believed or said about the mind is false. It is a robotic maker of mental images.

The following statement resonates with my definition.

> A truth's initial commotion is directly proportional to how deeply the lie was believed. It wasn't the world being round that agitated people, but that the world wasn't flat. When a well-packaged web of lies has been sold gradually to the masses over generations, the truth will seem utterly preposterous and its speaker a raving lunatic. (Dresden James quotes, 2005)

No! I am not a raving lunatic, and neither are the many individuals who have been trained in the use of my methods to help others, such as John Avery, who wrote the following:

> *From John Avery, who has more than 30 years' experience as a Counselor/Practitioner*
>
> When I was first introduced to the concept that the only function of our mind is the creation of a mental image picture of anything we have our attention on, I

was skeptical, because the idea flew in the face of all my earlier training.

I now know this concept to be fact, from my own personal experience as a client, then as a trained practitioner introducing this fact to some hundreds of clients in the past five years.

This truth, along with the Mace Energy Method, has allowed me to be able to really help clients take charge of their lives.

Life was not meant to be complicated; this is a simple (easy to prove) but powerful fact.

Neither are there raving lunatics among the hundreds of clients who have benefited from the research. One such client wrote:

I've been trying to write to you for a while. Wanting to let you know how I am since you helped me. It's strange – for a long time I couldn't really put it into words. Actually, I'm not sure I can now, but I'd like to give it a whirl.

Well, I'm happier. Settled. Calmer. Mostly I feel that I am a better person. That sounds kind of lame, and yet it is the best way for me to describe how I feel. When I asked my husband if he noticed any difference in me he said that I appear calmer to him and that I am softer and that there is much more of Mary present.

It wasn't a big fireworks type of thing. I didn't want to scream from the rooftops or jump up and down for joy. I've been through those types of highs before – seen them come and go. I am much more impressed by the quiet, subtle shift from misery and halting ridge-iness towards life, to a silent, calm acceptance and peace within. To a joyful outlook, to eyes that see the beauty in things instead of looking for the ugliness and the 'wrong'.

In a nutshell – the help you gave me has been life changing. I have a better quality of life because of what you did.

It seems absurd to say thank you for such a thing... but thank you very, very, very much.

Exploring definitions of the mind

When you consider the mind's totally abstract, totally intangible quality, the lack of a finite definition is perfectly understandable, for it is extremely difficult to define something that has no substance. Understanding this, however, does not change anything. We all know the mind exists from our own subjective observations, which give it subjective – although not objective – reality. So its nature is generally considered an enigma. My own research and case histories have thrown new light on the subject of the mind: what it is, what it is not, how it operates, and its purpose. For me, the mind is no longer an enigma.

Until the advent of the concept of identities, there were only three components in conventional wisdom concerning the human species: *mind, body* and *spirit* (see Chapter 1). As *identities* are independent of all three, they do not form part of the following discussion.

The mind has been the subject of much writing and conjecture by philosophers for thousands of years. Millions of words 'appear' to be have been written about it. The word 'appear' is used advisedly, as very little is ever written about the mind per se, although conventional teachings and beliefs imply otherwise. However, when conventional teachings and beliefs are taken into account, there is an implication that this is the case. In particular, whenever the subjects of non-optimum behavior, emotional problems and emotional disorders are discussed, the term *mental illness* is used. As stated in Chapter 1, emotional conditions have nothing to do with the mind, but are simply the products of negative identities, and therefore the term 'mental illness' is a complete misnomer.

Everything that occurs must have a source. To my knowledge, the human spirit has never been named as the source of, and blamed for, any of the behavioral shortcomings or emotional ills of humans, so we are left with the two other components of the triumvirate, body and mind.

In certain scientific circles there is the idea that the brain has intellectual properties, that it is the brain that does the thinking and, in particular, the storing of knowledge. Our language is full of sayings that promote this concept, for example 'She is very brainy', or the rather derogatory 'All brawn and no brain!' The epitome of this theory is demonstrated by the preservation of the brains of Einstein and other great thinkers for clinical study! This is the extreme of materialism, for it totally ignores the spirit, and reduces sentient beings such as Einstein to material objects, although atheists apparently accept it without question.

The most significant question materialists have been unable to answer relates to the ability of an individual to store prodigious amounts of knowledge and operate as an intellectual, and thinking, sentient life form. That is a conundrum that will never be solved, because there is no answer. All the abilities assigned to the brain (and for that the matter the mind) are the abilities of the *being*, the spirit, and the life force. This will be elaborated upon later.

To put to rest any ideas that the brain has an intellectual ability, consider this: if you had the opportunity to compare the brain of a large ape with the brain of a human, you would find there is not much difference in size. Even if the human brain were twice the size of that of an ape, you certainly could not equate the difference in size alone with the vast difference in the intelligence of the two species, yet the brains of both are composed of the same material – pinkish grayish colored nervous tissue. Additionally, the same tissue of which the brain is composed extends down the spine, where it is called the spinal cord. In the light of this, how is it that thought and memory do not emanate from the spine, but only from the nervous tissue in the head! The brain is a part of the body, as is the leg, heart or liver, so what special qualities does the brain have that are not present in the other body organs, particularly in the brain's extension, the spinal cord?

To introduce a little levity at this point, what follows is a short parody posted to an Internet discussion group some years ago. It was quite topical at the time, which is why I retained a copy.

Imagine if you will… the leader of an Intergalactic Exploration Team reporting to his commander after returning from a visit to planet Earth.

Leader: The Earth people are made out of meat.

Commander: Meat?

Leader: Meat. They are made out of meat.

Commander: Meat?

Leader: There is no doubt about it. We picked up several species of different color and took them aboard. We probed them all the way through. They are completely made of meat on a bone framework.

Commander: That's impossible! What about the radio signals? The signals were definitely from Earth.

Leader: They use radio waves to communicate, but the signals do not come from them. They come from machines.

Commander: So who made the machines? That is whom you should have contacted.

Leader: *They* made the machines! That is what I am trying to tell you! Meat made the machines!

Commander: That's ridiculous. How can meat make machines? You are asking me to believe in sentient meat – have you been on the glastos again?

Leader: No sir. I have not touched a drop since that last episode. But I am telling you; those Earth creatures that control the planet are all made of meat.

Commander: You are sure the ones you got were not mutating through a meat stage?

Leader: No, they are born that way and die that way. They are meat all through, apart from the bone structure.

Commander: What, no controlling core?

Leader: Oh. They have a core all right. They call it a brain. It's in their head. But that is only meat too.

Commander: So, what does the thinking?

Leader: The brain of course. It controls their bodies. Without the head they immediately die.

Commander: What are you telling me?

Leader: I am telling you that the brain appears to do the thinking.

Commander: You are telling me that there is such a thing as thinking meat!

Leader: Yes. Thinking meat. Sentient meat... and I have not been on the glastos!

Apart from the above parody, logic puts the brain

where it belongs, a 'meat' component of the body with no intellectual properties. These properties must reside elsewhere. Logic tells me that the brain is just a part of the body, and that it is the organ at the centre of the body's nervous system. The brain is the apparent source of our bodily or muscular functions, and rightly belongs in the field of physiology, but what activates the brain is another matter altogether.

The false attribution of emotional and behavioral problems to the mind is reinforced when you consult a dictionary, for no finite definition of *mind* exists in any of the dictionaries at my disposal. The two-volume *The World Book Dictionary* gives 17 versions of 'mind', but refers to it as: '*That which does*'. A definition of *that*, however, is not provided! Another prestigious dictionary, *The American Heritage Dictionary*, in almost as many versions, refers to it as: '*the seat of intellect, the source of emotions...*' Another large dictionary, *The Australian Oxford Dictionary*, has similar versions, but once again does not define what it is, only what it is believed to do. The dictionaries talk about function, albeit erroneously, but not structure.

Defining psychology and spirit

The suffix *Ology* refers to a branch of knowledge, and the word *psyche* is Greek for *spirit* or *life*. Thus psychology in its original and logical meaning referred to a study or knowledge of the human spirit, and it remained thus until the middle of the nineteenth century.

In 1856, Wilhelm Wundt, a medical student,

graduated from Heidelberg University and joined the staff in the psychology department, where he remained for 17 years. Later, he created laboratories to study human behavior and helped to give psychology a new definition. His ideas spawned present-day psychology – a study of the mind, as distinct from a study of the spirit. One of Wundt's students, James Mark Baldwin, is credited with introducing the changed definition – what is now known as a 'study of the mind' or a 'study of human behavior' (Lionni & Klass, 1980). Wundt apparently saw no point in engaging in and continuing the apparently endless discussion concerning the nature of the psyche. Being of a more practical bent, he decided that behavior was something that was quantifiable – you cannot see the mind or the spirit, but behavior is very observable, so it could be classified. His branch of psychology, therefore, ignored the psyche. What the source of human behavior was attributed to before Wundt I do not know, but it is a fair guess that it was, correctly, not attributed to the psyche, hence the need for a new definition excluding that word.

It is very easy to be wise after the event, but what seems obvious now is that the mind was (and still is) confused with the psyche, hence Wundt's easy transition in thinking.

Thinking in pictures

Although I have never considered the brain to have an intellectual capacity, it has to be admitted that when

I started my own research I was of the opinion that the mind thought in pictures. I was as confused as everyone else as to the precise but disparate roles of mind and spirit.

Researchers often find answers to problems they were not addressing, and I fall into that category. I did not arrive at an understanding of the mind's true role and function by logical thinking, but when an answer to something you were not even pondering suddenly appears, it is worth exploring, no matter how much it challenges sacred beliefs.

The truth about the mind is going to be contentious in the extreme, and may well invite the rejoinder 'That is your opinion!' My response is that the world is full of opinions, but none of them has any bearing on what is true. The truth is what it is, and all the divergent and opposing opinions in the world will not change it.

The mind is an abstract and intangible entity. The spirit creates it in order to play a game in the physical universe – to facilitate the game of life. In this regard it is indispensable. The spiritual being does the thinking, stores knowledge and makes decisions, and the mind creates pictures to match the being's thoughts. Here is an example of this vital function. A person has a dream of what they would like to happen in the future. The dream is a nebulous idea –without substance – of what that person envisages for the future. Now that the being has its attention on the dream, the mind dutifully but robotically creates a mental image to represent it.

Thus *the first step in enabling the dream to become a reality is the creation of a mental image to represent it.*

In the same way, imagine you are looking at your car, standing dirty and unpolished in the driveway. Not being content with it like that, you mentally envisage it as clean and shiny. As this is what you are thinking, your mind produces the image of the clean and shiny car. The image is the first step in making a clean and shiny car a reality, but the car will remain dirty and unpolished until you decide to do something about it. How you bring your image of a clean car into reality does not matter. You can take it to a car wash, ask a son or daughter to wash and polish it, or take out a hose to do it yourself. The principle is that *nothing appears in the physical universe that does not appear in someone's mental universe first.* This is the sequence: first the dream, then the mental image, and then the reality occurring, when some energy has been applied to achieving the dream.

The examples are endless. Every invention starts out as a dream, a nebulous idea with no substance, but aimed at solving a problem of some kind, such as the Wright brothers' dream of heavier than air flight, or Marconi's dream of telegraphic communication. The former saw birds in flight, but Marconi had only his dream, with, as far as I am aware, nothing tangible as inspiration.

The first definitive step is the appearance of a mental image of a solution; the first rung on the ladder to achieving the goal appears as a mental image in the mind of the inventor. No matter how many examples you use, the answer is always the same: *the physical reality is always preceded by the mental image of that reality.* The engineer Eiffel, who designed the famous tower in Paris, conceived the idea and then employed other engineers to help make it a reality. He had a dream of a large tower, and gradually the concept developed into a mental image of what he would build.

Apart from illustrating the mind's vital role in the game of life, the above examples also indicate the mind's role in creating mental pictures of the spiritual being's focus.

The mind, spirit and pictures

Spiritual beings in their native state have neither a body nor a mind. It appears that the mind is created spontaneously with the creation of the body, for it is as much a tool for playing a game in the physical universe as the body. You nearly got it right Mr. Wundt, but it is the mind that is devoid of self-determinism, not the spirit. The mind reacts to stimuli from the self-determined spirit. When a person's body tells them that it is hungry, and their attention is focused on food, their mind creates a picture of food, but only as a response to the focus on food. That is precisely how the mind functions! *It manifests pictures of whatever the being's attention is focused on.* If you say to someone 'Think about a football match,' or 'Think about going to the movies,' these are perfect cues for the mind to manifest relevant pictures. Try the following to see how it works.

Think of an elephant.

Think of a dentist.

Think of a friend.

Think of your bed.

Think of an apple.

In quick succession as you read, you will have created different mental images: pictures of an elephant, a dentist, your friend, your bed and an apple. You may consciously decide to focus your attention on something else, but initially your mind will respond by creating the relevant pictures. It is apparent that the mind is devoid of self-determinism; it is a stimulus–response mechanism.

The same result would have materialized, of course, if the instruction had been *not* to think about football or *not* to think about going to the movies. This highlights a very important point: one cannot *not think* about anything. This is an incredibly important component in the model that has been created to develop personal happiness, loving relationships and the eradication of emotional problems. To emphasize the point that you cannot *not think* of something, do the following.

DO NOT think of an elephant.
DO NOT think of a dentist.

DO NOT think of a friend.

DO NOT think of your bed.

DO NOT think of an apple.

It is ironical that if you say 'Do not think of something,' the mind produces a picture of that something. Why? Because your attention has moved to that 'something'. Logically, the mind produces that something to illustrate what *not to think about*. If, for example, a person is told, 'Do not think about it,' they will not create a mental image and will make the natural response, 'Do not think about what?' When told, 'Do not think about your bedroom,' they will immediately create an image of their bedroom. Crazy, I know, but then the mind, like a computer, cannot rationalize. It is an unthinking robot at the behest of the being. It has no control over the mental images it creates. This illustrates and emphasizes its function as a stimulus–response mechanism, and that it does not do any thinking.

The ability of the mind to picture past events automatically is another fact of inestimable value in the life-enhancement procedures developed by my research.

My original conclusion involved the mind as a mechanism that thought in pictures, but that was just a step on the way. Further analysis, experience and research indicate that this is not so. If told, 'Think about a football match,' it is apparent that the instruction is really, '*you* think about a football match.' This un-stated word, *you*, is the crux of the realization about the relationship between spirit and mind. Although, in any conversation, it is *you* who is being addressed, this is never stated. The important point that is easily overlooked is that the person is talking to *you*, not your mind. The prime action is *you*, the spiritual being, focusing your attention on the football match. The secondary action is the mind producing a relevant mental image, even if only with a nanosecond of delay, too short to be noticeable. It is not a case of, '*Mind*, think about football,' it is, '*you*, think about football.'

Each human body is unique and visible as a material object composed of bone and flesh. Each person's mind is similarly unique, but invisible to outside observers. Therefore, as the mind is invisible to others, it is not an external object. Given this, it is esoteric in the fullest sense – totally private and confidential. It is a subjective entity. Although the mind is invisible and intangible, it nevertheless has the ability to create pictures, mental images that *are* observable, and are thus subjective realities. We observe the mental images that our minds create.

We now must ask: what is the purpose of creating mental pictures? Providing the answer to this question is important in understanding the fabulous and indispensable mechanism of the mind. Eiffel and his tower are an example of one of the mind's uses, but to expand upon the concept of mental images, the desktop computer is a perfect tool.

Mind and monitor

A practical example of this is that as I sit here now, typing this manuscript, the computer monitor keeps a visual record of every word and every symbol, in fact the entire context of what I am composing, while at the same time recording it in the hard drive – the computer's memory. If I did not have the visual display of the monitor, I would have no indication of what has been stored in the memory or deleted, until I printed it out; I would only have my memory of the particular keys I pressed. To make this more real to those readers who use a computer, next time you write something, turn off the monitor and then continue writing! It would be blithely naïve to expect to make no mistakes during the initial writing, but they would not be apparent until the printout stage – which would make editing a veritable nightmare!

In a similar vein, imagine the difficulty encountered in creating a complicated computer program without the benefit of visualizing it in the process of development. More pertinently, without the monitor, the facility of graphic computer displays would be non-existent. *Mind* is almost synonymous with *monitor*, although the other way around is probably more factual.

The spirit and the mind are so close in apparent nature that they can be argued to be one and the same. Each is invisible, intangible and totally abstract. Such close proximity makes the confusion between the two very understandable, but does not alter their function as separate entities. Their separateness is emphasized in the next section.

The mind is totally abstract and intangible, yet has material universe duplication in the monitor of a desktop computer. Additionally, both *body* and *spirit* also have their counterparts in that device. To complete the duplication, some anti-social individual also created the computer virus, which is a perfect duplication of a negative identity.

The diagram below indicates the duplication of mind, body and spirit. The negative identity and the virus are left un-illustrated, yet are parallel components.

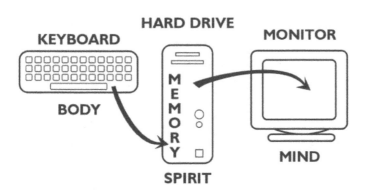

In expanding upon the monitor/mind comparison, the first thing to be noted is that the mind stores no knowledge and the monitor stores no data. The monitor is inherently blank, and without a connection to a computer program remains blank, even when connected to a power source. Any imagery it creates is derived from data in the hard drive. According to my reasoning and research, the mind is also inherently blank, but creates imagery according to the information it receives from the being.

The word 'memory' refers to stored information, so it is obvious how the term was adopted as computer jargon. The hard drive stores all computer data and the spirit stores all knowledge, hence the hard drive and the spirit are parallel. The keyboard parallels the body, for just as it activates stored hard-drive data, the body activates a being's knowledge.

The mind creates an image of whatever the person's attention is focused on. It changes images as a direct consequence of a change of attention by the individual – in other words, it follows the being's line of thought. Whenever the body's sensors trigger the being's knowledge, the mind produces an image of what has been accessed. Similarly, when the keyboard accesses data stored in the hard drive, the computer monitor produces images to represent the data being accessed. The identical roles of the keyboard and the body need an in-depth explanation, for this is the salient, but not obvious, point.

Remembering is the act of bringing knowledge into conscious recall. All recall is the result of tapping into knowledge, and the vehicle used is the body's sensor. The body has innumerable sensors – sound, touch, smell, taste and sight being the major ones, but I have seen a list of about 50. Fundamentally, a sensor is a detector, a detector of what is happening around or in the body; it makes a person aware of what is happening within their body as well as in their immediate environment. It is easy to forget that this is the basic function of bodily sensors.

The touch or tactile sensor gives a message to the brain, via nerve channels, that the body is in direct contact with something or, for example, that it detects some radiated heat. The fingertips are very sensitive to texture, and a person with their eyes closed while fingering the texture or shape of something can easily recognize what it is. This, of course, only applies if the person has previously seen or felt the object in question – its various physical properties have been recorded as knowledge. An example of this is Braille, by which a blind person is able to *read* by using the sensors in the fingertips to recognize the meaning of various small shapes. This allows the blind person to access information via the tactile senses rather than the visual senses. The result is that the person has acquired information, irrespective of the channel used.

Another practical example from my early days as a mariner is the, now probably forgotten, art of 'swinging the lead' to establish the depth of water into which a ship is venturing. The weighted line has a series of *marks* attached to it, each distinct from the other, for instance a small piece of leather with a hole in it, a piece of bunting, small lengths of cord with different numbers of knots tied in them. In daylight, the mark on the surface of the water indicates the depth; and in the dark the sailor swinging the lead can identify the mark by its texture or physical properties, and can quickly deduct the distance he is standing above the water. In practice, the sailor swinging the lead would

73

call out, 'By the mark so and so.' The prefix was said to alert the officer supervising that a reading was about to be voiced.

Using the sight sensor as an example, a person is made aware of the distance of their body from some other object. Sitting on the edge of a very tall building, the person is made aware of how high they are, with the resultant desire or compulsion to hang on tight if feeling apprehensive about heights. If this is the case, the sight sensor has triggered fear of heights, an example of secondary triggering.

The ears, as sound sensors, relay to the brain that there is something emanating sound waves and, from knowledge acquired, the source of the sound waves can be recognized. Every sensor triggers data in the person's memory bank. On hearing a dog barking, for instance, the hearing sensor may trigger knowledge of what type of dog it is that can be heard. There is no need to go into different types of dog barks, but what has happened is that stored knowledge has been accessed via the sound sensor.

Without mentioning other sensors, it is apparent that they all pass messages to the brain concerning the immediate environment, and there, in detail, is the explanation of the similarity between keyboard and body – each accesses memory/knowledge to produce images.

Limitations of computers

With the desktop computer, electronic engineers have simulated the function of human life on a very small scale, and have come as close as possible to duplicating life. The human spirit is unique in its ability to rationalize and think. I remember a philosophic discussion titled *the computer's ability to act independently*. To my amazement, the convener was adamant that computers were already capable of independent operation, and the time would come when they could operate totally independently of us: 'They can already turn themselves on and off... to a time schedule!' I will leave unsaid what his reaction was when I asked who created the program and who connected the computer to the power source.

Even if a computer could really think, you could *never* create a perfect duplicate of the human spirit. The word 'never' is used without question, because it is a physical impossibility to build a mechanical contrivance (a computer storage system such as the hard drive) with an infinite storage capacity. No matter how big or how efficient you make a mechanical contrivance, it always has a finite storage capacity – unlike the human spirit, which has an infinite storage capacity. Not only that, a being is energy, which makes it totally independent of any exterior source of energy, whereas a computer must be supplied with a source of energy, even if it is a self-contained solar panel. Science cannot completely duplicate or create life. The physical or material universe and the energy universe are two entirely different things.

The remaining example yet to be discussed is the virus/negative identity. Earlier, it was stated that a spiritual being is perfect in its own right and always invariably makes rational, optimum survival decisions about life unless the decisions are corrupted by negative identities. The computer is a life-enhancement tool, which always produces correct answers unless a virus has been incorporated into its system; once the virus starts functioning, the computer cannot produce valid answers. The inventor of the first virus was duplicating a negative identity, but was almost certainly not aware of what he was doing as regards duplicating a life function.

There is no doubt that the desktop computer is a most profound development in terms of its capacity to emulate the major aspects of life. Sentient beings operate via the concept of mind, body, spirit and identities, just as the computer operates with keyboard, hard drive, monitor and viruses.

The closer science's developments move towards simulating life, the more powerful is the *invention*. I suppose the difference between what I refer to, as my 'realisations' and 'inventions' is that inventions are of the physical universe, whereas realisations are of the energy universe.

The mind at birth

It is indisputable that the creation of the human body begins at the moment of conception. Further, it is quite probable that at this momentous point in time the mind is also created.

This concept is remarkably similar to the theory of some of the great philosophers, Hobbes, Hume, Locke and Berkley for example. They belonged to what is known as the Empiricists' school of thought, which advocated the idea that at birth the mind is a complete blank. It was described as empty of any data – *tabula rasa* – knowledge being acquired only as a result of experience, hence the title of their school of thought.

As a matter of interest, today's regression techniques, used in various forms of mental therapy, completely negate the theory that *birth* is the moment when the storing of knowledge commences. Although hypnotism has its detractors, particularly when it produces memory of past lives, there are far too many examples from different sources for these experiences to be ignored. Such is the case with the book *The Search for Bride Murphy* (Bernstein, 1956), which raised a furor as an account of Bride's alleged recovery under hypnotism of memory of past lives. As one who has both objective and subjective knowledge and experience of past lives, I take the data in the book at face value, although I am not an advocate of hypnotherapy.

From the Empiricists' concept of *tabula rasa*, two different theories emerge. First, if you are a believer in reincarnation, you may believe that the mind is permanent for the spiritual being, or energy unit, and is carried forward from one lifetime to the next. This would imply that the mind is cleared at death, so that it starts each incarnation with a clean slate. Second, and almost coincident with this theory, is the belief that the mind is created anew for each new lifetime or new body. There is a profound philosophic difference between the two theories, and I am not anchored in either, but for practical purposes either theory is acceptable as regards day-to-day existence.

My interest in the Empiricists' theory of the mind being blank at birth lies in the contention that blankness is not foreign to it. The mind's ability to be blank at any moment at all is the cornerstone of my own contention that it can and does go blank continually in its modus operandi.

My premise is that the mind automatically wipes itself clean the moment you transfer your attention from one thing to another. The image representing the original subject or area of attention goes, and is replaced by the image representing the new subject of attention. Underpinning this is the concept of the spiritual being as the sole storehouse of knowledge, the sole origin of thought, and the mind being purely a 'subjective reality' that mirrors the thoughts of the being.

To answer the skeptics of this claim, I ask these questions: 'What is knowledge?' 'Is it something that can be weighed?' 'Does it have color?' 'Does it have form?' These questions are not rhetorical, for they do require answers, and the answer to each is obviously 'No.' Knowledge is a completely abstract and intangible commodity. It is a form of energy that is invisible.

Data and knowledge

There is a fine line between data and knowledge. Data is something that is stored in archives, on tapes, on CDs, in computer hard drives and books and, in ancient times, carved in stone. It is derived from numerous sources in the written, spoken or illustrated form. Data becomes knowledge when stored away, ready to be accessed as memory. With the abstract and intangible nature of both knowledge and spiritual beings, it follows therefore that they are compatible. Just as a spoon of sugar can integrate and become one with a bowl of similar sugar, so is knowledge absorbed by a being. The only difference is that there is no limit to how much knowledge a being can absorb, for, unlike the bowl of sugar, it has no physical or material properties. This is a logical concept when you consider that in the case of a being and its knowledge, there is nothing material or tangible to store, only energy, which takes up no space. With this in mind, I have no trouble accepting that a being has an infinite capacity to store knowledge with which to compute, as and when needed.

The old-fashioned film projector used for enlarging transparencies on a screen makes an excellent analogy to illustrate the mind's function. In this analogy, the screen represents the mind and the projector represents a live body. Just as a body is activated by the energy of a spiritual being, the projector is activated by the energy from a light within it, so that the light in the projector represents the inherent energy of the being. The various memories and experiences, which are so important to the Empiricist theory, are represented by individual photographic slides. Experience, as a noun, means anything and everything that a person has undergone, from falling off a bicycle to learning to read. It is all stored away within the psyche and remains unexamined until the person recalls it by focusing his or her attention on it.

Let us examine the function of a film projector that uses photographic slides. A projector with no power connected to it is akin to a dead body – there is no energy source within – so the analogy is for a body inhabited by a life force and the projector with power connected and turned on.

When using the projector, the operator selects a slide, inserts it in the projector and then looks at the screen to view what is on the photographic slide. After viewing, he then removes the slide, and the screen goes blank until another slide is inserted. As often as this procedure is carried out, the screen will display an image, which changes according to the slides selected. The speed with which the slides are changed governs the length of time the screen is blank between slides. This is what happens in a movie camera: the movie film, which is a series of stills, changes so fast that there is no perceptible blank between the stills, so you have the illusion of movement. However, no matter what the illusion, there is a minuscule blankness between the stills.

Another analogy, and perhaps more in keeping with current photographic developments, is the digital camera, which can be connected directly to a television, allowing individual photographs to be displayed electronically when the camera's controls are manipulated. The time taken to manipulate the controls governs the periods of blankness on the television screen.

This is what happens in the spirit/mind relationship. When attention is focused on something, a mental image appears in your mind, in the same manner as the picture on a projector screen, or the television image from the camera. Focusing attention on something else is exactly the same as changing the slide in the projector or pressing 'next' on the digital camera – a different picture appears. Every time your attention changes, your mind produces a different picture for you to view, and the picture is entirely dependent on where your attention is focused. The mind must go blank between each take, just as in a movie, and, just as in a movie, you cannot perceive the blankness because it happens so quickly.

If you think about a dog, you see a picture of a dog. Now think about a horse. What has happened? The picture of the dog has gone and has been replaced by a picture of a horse. The first picture confirms that you were thinking about a dog, but the second picture confirms that your attention is now on a horse; each picture confirms that you have your attention in the right place!

All kinds of mental games are possible using the dog and the horse: the dog can walk up to the horse; the horse can walk up to the dog; the dog can jump on the horse's back; or all attention can be on the horse and the dog can be eliminated. The point is that some other picture concerning the horse has replaced the original mental picture of the dog. There is no way you can view the *original* picture of the dog and also include the horse. Each is a different picture in its own right and therefore there must be a minutely brief blank between one picture and the next. The mind goes blank or is wiped clean between mental pictures. The more you experiment with this concept, the more it is analogous to a projector, and the more it becomes apparent that the mind throws up pictures or mental images at the behest of the spiritual being. It is apparent that the Empiricists were on the right track with their concept of *tabula rasa*.

It is not only the past that can be visualized in the mind, but, as with Eiffel and his tower, also dreams of the future. Whether you are envisaging the past or the future, the self-same phenomenon occurs. When a person has a dream for the future, they use their mind to express the idea, their dream, in physical universe terms. Assume that in this dream for the future is a lovely weekend cottage. As the being adds details to the dream, such as the number of rooms, wall cladding, roof design and color etc., the concept is transferred onto the screen – the mind. Once again, it is not the mind that did the dreaming and envisaging, it is the being. The being used the mind to make pictures of its dreams. As stated earlier, the nebulous dream of a weekend cottage comes first and then the mind creates a picture as the dreamer envisages his or her creation.

It could be said that all mental images are an illusion, for they disappear once you stop applying energy to them (take your attention off them). This notion has a remarkable similarity to an Eastern philosophic contention that the physical universe is purely an illusion. This is borne out by accounts of people enjoying moments of high spiritual awareness, during which parts of their physical environment suddenly vanished. There may be more truth in this Eastern concept than is generally accorded.

To sum up, it is obvious that the mind is inherently blank, intangible and abstract. It may be argued that this is too simple a solution for such a serious subject as an understanding of the human mind, but why does it have to be complex? You may think it is too simple a solution for something that thinkers have pondered and argued over for centuries, but all problems have to be solved eventually, and it is amazing how simple the solutions often turn out to be. Usually, the more simple the solution, the greater its recognized worth. What is simpler than a wheel, but try to imagine civilization without that invention. We would not even have a wheelbarrow! The wheel derives its power from its simplicity.

Underpinning the theory concerning the mind is the

basic belief in the inherent spirituality of the human race. If your own spirituality were not real to you, you probably wouldn't have read this far. Considering this, it is fair to assume that as you are still reading, your own spiritual nature is to some extent real to you, and you may now have a better understanding of your own inherent qualities and your relationship to your mind.

The very fact that you can see the mental images you create indicates that they must have some substance – otherwise you could not see them. Having substance is another way of saying they have some mass, some material content, and as infinitely minuscule as that mass is, it does exist and you have created it. The image was not there before you focused your attention on something, so you must have created it. It could be said that you have created matter from nothing and, although it may appear that way, it is not the truth. The truth is that you have turned energy into matter, which is in line with scientific theory that nothing can be destroyed; you can only change its form.

The fact that the role of the mind is to display mental pictures, and in doing so creates mental mass, is the lynch pin behind the procedures developed in the Mace Energy Method. The incredible effectiveness of these procedures is testimony to this newfound, albeit revolutionary, truth regarding the true nature of the mind.

If you have any doubts about the veracity of what you have read, look at what happens in the creation of a human body. A minute spermatozoon from male semen enters an ovum in a female body (or a test tube) and from these two minuscule elements of life an incredibly complex and functional human body is created. If it was not for the resultant body that proves the event has taken place, how far fetched would the concept seem! Seeing believes of course, so I suggest you have a look at what has been happening to you and your mind as you have read this. Just analyze what you have seen, for seeing is *believing*!

The extent to which the erroneous understanding of the mind's role has totally permeated our culture is evident in our language with phrases such as, 'Mind over matter,' 'Be mindful,' 'His mind is made up,' 'When I make up my mind.' The fact, used in the fullest sense of the word, is that it is the being that is doing the deciding, not the mind. This indicates how much their relationship has been misunderstood; their independent roles and functions have been totally confused. Factually, the expression 'When I make up my mind' should be 'When I decide.'

The expression 'my mind' has another significance. When you say 'my' you are referring to yourself as an entity, and when you say 'my mind' you are claiming that the entity that is you possesses another entity, called your mind. Logic will tell you that the possessor is senior to, or superior to, the possessed, and that 'puts it in a nutshell'.

Healing emotional problems

We must now get to the 'nitty gritty': the importance of the mind's function in healing emotional problems. When it is said that the mind's only role is to create mental imagery, the word 'only' is in the context of this being its *sole* role.

As unbelievable as the new understanding of the mind's role may be, what has yet to be disclosed is another ability aligned with that role.

> The mind has the incredible ability to create a mental image to represent a concept, and what is a concept but an idea or notion. Harnessing this incredible ability is the pivotal factor in the emotional healing model that has evolved.

To make this real, consider this little scenario, in which Mary is explaining to Joan, her helper, how she wants something done. It is not straightforward and requires some detailed explanation. Mary is inclined to be a bit verbose and commences to provide much unnecessary detail. Before she has completed her explanation, Joan interrupts with this comment, 'Okay Mary, I've got the picture!' What she is actually saying is that she understands what Mary wants. Mary's idea of what she wants Joan to do is a concept or notion, and when Joan in turn understands what Mary wants, it means that she understands the concept and gets a mental picture of it. This is a very common, everyday expression indicating understanding. Every one of us, since time immemorial, has been utilizing that aspect of the mind's function without realizing it.

Love is a very 'high' human emotion, manifested in many ways. When thinking of what it means, disassociated from any explanations or examples, the mind will create a mental image to represent it. The nature of the image is immaterial; but no matter what the image is, it represents love to you. If, while reading this last paragraph, you have received no image, just close your eyes and think of *what love means to you.* You will receive an image of something. Then close your eyes again, go to the other end of the emotional scale, and think of *what hate means to you.* You will receive another, but different, mental image. To make this function of your mind real to you, next think of what *anger means to you.* Another, different, image will appear.

Love, hate and anger are concepts. Your mind has created images to represent them because you have understood what they mean. I trust that any skepticism you may have harbored has now been dissipated!

All negative identities, as discussed in Chapters 1 and 2, are concepts, irrespective of their content. Not one of the identities has a material component. You cannot see fear, loneliness, abandonment, feelings of inadequacy, or any of the other myriad negative ideas and feelings that comprise negative identities – they are all concepts. They all manifest actions and feelings, but the identities per se are invisible, because they are simply *energy.* No matter what their content, they are *energy ridges.*

A very important factor has to be remembered

here. *The mind has absolutely no intellectual properties!* It is a robotic stimulus–response mechanism, and when someone understands a concept, the image it creates will be anything from a donut to a dinosaur, an ice cream to an elephant! Naturally enough, no matter how thoroughly it is explained, new clients are invariably amazed at what they find themselves looking at.

To clarify how the mind functions, do this: draw something! No, I am not going to tell you what to draw; you decide. How many millions of things are there for you to choose from? That is what the mind is confronted with, except it has no intellectual power, no power of choice, as you have, so it just willy-nilly produces a picture, which can be anything.

I have a special filing system for all clients, and it is housed in my waste paper basket! This is not really a joke, for no client's session records are ever retained. Once the unwanted identities have gone, no purpose is achieved by retaining them. Delving into the basket, it is found that the morning client produced images of a Japanese man, a brick wall and a tree to represent the three identities mentioned. If you can find anything more irrational than that, it would be interesting to know what it is!

Truth is indeed stranger than fiction! This new concept of the mind is so incredible that it may seem incomprehensible; however, it is as factual as it may seem unreal.

Today's materialistic researchers, in ignoring the

spiritual component of the mind, body and spirit triumvirate, and being unable to find answers within the mind, are now postulating that the *body* is the source of these emotional maladies. Intriguingly, however, they are still referred to as 'mental illness'. What is overlooked is that the body is only feeling and dramatizing the effects of energy, in the same manner as a television manifests a picture as a result of the energy transmitted through the ether by a TV station.

If the energy impinging on the body is negative, the body responds with, for example, grief, and subsequently tears; but if the energy is positive, the body will respond with, say, laughter. The energy's frequency governs the mood level it creates: the higher the frequency, the higher the mood level.

All positive energies emanate from the spirit or human energy unit, for spiritual beings are naturally optimistic. But negative energies emanate from unknowingly created negative identities, alter egos or substitute selves. How they are dis-created is the subject of Chapter 7.

CHAPTER 4

Time and the universes

The new, and in many cases unique body of knowledge embraced in this book is called *Causism*. This is an expression developed to differentiate the work from other fields of thought and practice. In arriving at the name, the elitism of Greek and Latin roots was shunned in favor of more commonly understood Anglo-Saxon terminology. It is defined thus:

> *Causism* is a new body of knowledge, a new philosophy of life. Its name is derived from: (1) *cause*: to create an effect; to make things happen; and (2) *ism*: a doctrine, system or principle.

> Causism is very much a practical philosophy, for in addition to its revolutionary principles, it embodies an equally revolutionary practical component called the *Mace Energy Method*, which promotes this mission

90

statement: **to assist people to be in control of their lives and live their own dreams.**

It is from this statement that the term Causism was adopted, for the words 'cause' and 'control' are synonymous.

The graduates who are trained in Causism are Mace Energy Method Practitioners.

Time

As stated in Chapter 1, we are made up of energy, and every person living on planet Earth is activated by a unit of energy that Causism calls a human energy unit. Causism is entirely devoid of any religious connotations; it is a scientific examination of life. To reinforce that concept, and despite the potential for controversy, the more scientific term *energy unit*, rather than the religiously derived *spiritual being*, is preferred. While Causism is not connected to any religious thinking, the term *spiritual being*, nevertheless, is widely used herein, because it is widely used, accepted and understood in our culture.

Logics are a system of rational thought developed by Aristotle, the Greek philosopher, in approximately 350 BC. From this, the term *logical thinking* developed. For those unfamiliar with his philosophic teaching, Aristotle devised what he called *syllogisms*, where two known or accepted truths, called *premises*, are used to establish a third truth. Here is an often-used example.

Premise 1. All people are mortal.

Premise 2. He is a person.

Conclusion. He is mortal.

Here is another syllogism.

Premise 1. All spiritual beings are immortal.

Premise 2. Tom is a spiritual being.

Conclusion. Tom is immortal!

The very logical thinking expounded by Aristotle tells us there is something wrong with this conclusion, because we know that Tom is not immortal; he will eventually die. It is not Aristotelian logic that is wrong; what is wrong is the second premise, for *Tom* is a composite: being + body. (This will be elaborated on later.) The being is of the energy universe but the body is of the physical or material universe, and what is happening is that the physical universe is being confused with the energy universe, where a different set of laws prevails. To express it differently, material universe logics (Aristotelian) are different from energy universe logics.

The energy universe is senior to the physical universe, for, as claimed by Causism and expounded later; the latter is a product of the former. It is interesting that the deeper the researchers of quantum physics research, the closer they are to the basis of the entire universe, *energy*. This is why recent research in quantum physics has started to raise doubts about some of the accepted ideas of Newton and even Einstein. Quantum physics research, moving ever nearer to basics, is encroaching or drifting more into the energy universe, away from the logics of the material universe, where the logics of Newton and Einstein are more germane.

The difference in the logics of the physical universe compared with the logics of the energy universe is very important. The Mace Energy Method, in addressing beings and not bodies, utilizes the logics of the energy universe, and not the logics of the material universe. Before proceeding further, we need to examine the enigma called time and ask, 'what is this commodity called time? Is it objective or subjective? Is it fact or fancy?'

The nature of time has been discussed, theorized and argued over by many great thinkers. One of the earliest I am aware of was Zeno, the Greek philosopher of about 450 years BC, who contended that time was 'in the mind' – in other words, it was purely a subjective reality. In more recent times, the German philosopher Emmanuel Kant (1724–1804) and his English counterpart Herbert Spencer (1820–1903) exemplified the divergent views held in academia concerning this 'commodity' called time.

Kant, as with the Greek philosopher Zeno, asserted that *time* (and *space*) was purely a subjective reality – that *time* and *space* was not objective; they were realities only in the consciousness of the individual. Spencer (Spencer, 1937) argued against this doctrine. In the foreword to this edition he is rightly described as a man of gigantic intellect, which he obviously was, but, as with many before and since, he was not correct about everything. He used logic to *prove* that time was an objective reality, and not a subjective reality. He was, of course, using material universe logic to address an energy universe concept, and, as in the syllogism above concerning Tom's immortality, the conclusion is not valid. He also concluded that although objective, time was *wholly incomprehensible*. These two words indicate the confusion that Spencer experienced despite his own logical *proof*. Such is the confusion that exists within individuals, never mind among groups, and the chasm that separates intellectual thinking or philosophic thought on the subject of time.

One highly regarded dictionary of the English language, *The American Heritage Dictionary*, describes time as '*A nonspatial continuum...*' – quite a mouthful, even without the remainder of the definition – but it is the only dictionary I have seen that attempts to define time rather than simply giving examples of how the word is used.

Einstein is famous for his Atomic Energy equation and also his Theory of Relativity, of which an essential component is *time*. Who, however, has heard of Count Alfred Korzybski? He was a member of an old Polish aristocratic family who had for generations been scientists, mathematicians and engineers. He trained as an engineer, and was well versed in mathematics.

After the First World War, during which he saw service on the General Staff of the Polish Army, he migrated to America, where he founded the Institute of General Semantics and wrote and lectured extensively until his death, aged 70, in 1951.

While many philosophers have written of time, motion, energy (force) and matter, my readings reveal that none has made the ultimate connection that Korzybski did, so we will examine what Korzybski contributed with Aristotelian logic. No doubt conditioned by his background in engineering and mathematics, he approached the conundrum of time from a practical perspective, or perhaps, like the ancient Greek philosopher Pythagoras, from a mathematical perspective.

In *Science and Sanity*, Korzybski (Korzybski, 1933) made an observation concerning time. His observation, which was an incidental reference used to make another point, forms the basis of the following exercise, which expands upon this observation and provides some food for thought regarding the commodity called time. Those with an enquiring nature will be particularly interested in the exercise. If you decide to do it, do not read further until you can sit quietly and be undisturbed for, say, 30 minutes. You will need a pen, or pencil, and paper to write on. When ready to continue, keep the rest of this writing covered by a piece of paper and only expose one paragraph at a time, for there follows a series of questions. Write down your own answers before proceeding, for my answers appear in the next and subsequent paragraphs. Doing it this way, you will be using your own data instead of mine, and any conclusions you arrive at will be yours. The questions are mine, but the answers will be yours. Of course, if you decide to look and see what my answers are, you will be using my data rather than your own.

This approach is based on the education system used by Socrates, who was renowned for asking questions instead of lecturing, thereby bringing out people's inherent knowledge. This is called *heuristic teaching*. It is the ultimate form of education, but its impractical aspects are obvious, and it would be a luxury in today's education system. But it is perfect for this exercise.

To commence the exercise, make a list of all the examples that create awareness of time passing. The obvious one is the clock, but you should endeavour to list between five and ten other examples, although if you can think of twenty or more, all the better. It does not matter how mundane or abstract the items are, as long as they indicate the passage of time. Keep the next paragraph covered until you are satisfied with your list.

Having done that, examine your list and compare it with the items I have chosen, which are only some of the ones I could have used: a working clock, a shadow changing place, the sun traversing the sky, the moon doing likewise, grass growing, trees growing, children growing, and a horse race. As you can see, we are not interested in how fast there is change, but simply that there is change. The change evident in a tree's growth is very slow compared with the speed of horses racing, or the hands of a clock going round.

No matter how many items you put on your list,

provided they indicate the passing of time, they will all have a single common factor, and it will be common to my list as well as yours.

Once again, keep the next paragraph covered until you are quite sure you have found the common factor.

The common factor is *motion* – be it the hands of an operating clock, the grass getting longer, and the sun moving in the sky or simply someone taking a journey. Every indication of time has motion, for what is known, as 'time' is totally dependent on motion. No motion leaves you with *nowness*. To labor the point, if the hands of the clock stop at 3.30, all you know is that it is no longer 3.30, and you can only guess at the time: no hands moving, no indication of time! Make sure you are 100% happy with this before looking at the next paragraph.

There are three essential components of motion. The next task is to write them down. Here is a clue: time is not one of them, for time is more of a bystander, whereas motion takes place. If the answers do not come easily, make a real effort to find them, but if you have to look at the next paragraph, so be it. I have sat with someone for as long as 30 minutes while they worked out the answers. Some people discover all three easily, but most people have trouble with at least one of them, although there is no particular one that predominates as the most difficult. You may, however, have no trouble at all.

The three essential components of motion are: matter, energy and space.

If you have written 'objects' or 'physical material' instead of 'matter', or 'force' instead of 'energy', that is fine, for we are not here to quibble over words. For the benefit of those who did not find the components for themselves I will explain, again using the rather commonplace clock face as an example.

The hands of the clock are matter, driven by an energy source (be it a spring or a battery) and require space in which to move. If the battery goes flat or the spring winds down, there is no energy and the clock stops – in other words, the hands cease to move. To sum up: *for motion to occur you need matter to move, energy to move it, and space for it to move in.*

Okay. If motion is an essential component of time, what happens to time if you take away matter? Of course! Without anything to move, there can be no motion, and without motion there is no time! Likewise, if you delete space but leave energy and matter, once again time does not exist. It is worth noting at this point that we are not concerned with the source of the energy, or how space came into existence, but simply with the fact that they exist. Space is, of course, easily explained: it is the absence of matter.

One last question before dispensing with the need to cover up succeeding paragraphs: 'Of what is the physical universe composed?'

The answer is of course: matter, energy and space.

Now consider this: if there is no matter (the physical component of the universe) and you are left with the void of space, can there be motion? The answer is obviously 'No'. If there is no motion, can there be time? Once again the answer is obviously 'No'. Now, if there is 'no time', you must have *timelessness*, which is another word for *eternity* – and where have you heard that word before?

I will now tell you what Korzybski wrote in his book *Science and Sanity*.

As stated earlier, he was making another point, so I paraphrase what he wrote for simplicity. If, to give someone the time, you hand them your watch, you are simply giving them matter moving through space, and that is the simplicity of it (Korzybski, 1933, p. 225): *According to what we know in 1933, the universe is 'time'-less; in other words, there is no such 'object' as 'time'* (p. 232).

Time is simply a subjective reality that cannot be felt, seen, heard or tasted. Yet, by observing and utilizing motion, we are able to measure it, or, to be more precise, measure its passing and give it a sense of objectivity. But it is only motion in some form that makes us cognizant of its apparent existence.

From the above logical argument, it would seem that Kant was correct and, despite his 'gigantic intellect', Spencer was incorrect, but it took Korzybski, an engineer, to prove it.

Time seems to slow down with pain and speed up with pleasure. This is another feature of time that helps confirm its true nature, as asserted by Kant and fellow thinkers. Whether we measure its passage with the ancient sundial or a digital clock, we know it just marches inexorably onward and that it rules our lives (if we let it!).

If you did not find your own answers in the above exercise, you may be skeptical about the conclusion that time does not really exist, and that it only *appears* to exist as a product of motion, a subjective reality with no substance. This is perfectly understandable. Some years ago, I gave this exercise to a very good friend of mine and insisted he supply all the answers, which he eventually did. Two weeks later he came to me and I have never forgotten his words: 'I cannot fault your argument John, but it is too simple a solution for such a serious subject!' He could not fault it, of course, because I had told him nothing! I had simply put the questions to him. All the data were his own, so how *could* he fault it! The concept was so incredible that even faced with a conclusion drawn from his own data, he was having trouble accepting it.

Finally, the idea of heaven from my early Christian upbringing is that it is a place we go to after death, at the moment of resurrection. To me, it was beyond credibility that you could go to heaven, because after death it was obvious, from an understanding of cremation and bodily decay, that there was no body to take there. Of course, my teachers didn't know, or, to be kind, forgot to mention, that *we* are not bodies, but *spiritual beings, energy units,* inhabiting bodies, and it was not our bodies that go to heaven, if such a place exists, but us.

The concept of *timelessness* casts a new light on the concept of heaven, so I leave you to ponder heaven, hell and eternity, if you have not already done so.

Universes

Causism postulates three universes: the energy universe, the material or physical universe, and our own personal universe. I have yet to see the term *energy universe*, classified or labeled as such, in any other writings or in any of the dictionaries at my disposal, so it is fair to say that it is a coined expression peculiar to this research.

Energy is invisible and therefore the energy universe is invisible, but it permeates the entire universe and, because we are energy units ourselves, that is our natural home. The material universe is basically everything that has substance, but, intriguingly, it creates that nebulous notion called *time*, which Spencer labeled a commodity. The third universe, *our own universe*, is composed of *everything of which we are aware*, including an awareness of self, all our personal knowledge and, importantly, an awareness of the other two universes.

I will leave you to decide the order of importance or magnitude of each of these three universes. My work is a scientific examination of all three, but is predominantly concerned with our own universe and its relationship with the other two. It could also be said to be a scientific examination of the spiritual or energy component of the human species. Only atheists dispute the fact that we are immortal human beings, but unless they deny the fact that we are energy, which is indestructible, they can hardly dispute that we are indeed immortal. It would appear that atheists, in rejecting the spiritual nature of human beings, are doing so because it is aligned with religious doctrines. It is probably the rejection of these doctrines that clouds their judgment!

The emotional healing model, the Mace Energy Method, the practical offshoot of Causism, owes its incredible success to recognizing and utilizing the difference between the logics (laws) of the energy universe and the logics (laws) of the material universe. The laws of the energy universe are different from the laws of the material universe, and the primary law of the energy universe is that it contains no time! In a nutshell, the phenomena of one universe cannot be computed with the logics of another!

The differences in these two logics are of incalculable importance, for the Mace Energy Method addresses beings (energy units) and not bodies. This has created an entirely new paradigm in addressing and resolving emotional problems.

CHAPTER 5

The real you

How often have you heard people say, 'I'll believe it when I see it'? The atheist, the supreme skeptic, the supreme materialist, a person who has no belief in the spiritual nature of human beings and therefore no awareness of their own spirituality, epitomizes the saying 'Show me and I will believe you.'

When addressing the subject of spirituality, the inability to 'see it' is probably the greatest impediment there is to enabling people to recognize their own true nature as spiritual beings, for there is, in all truth, nothing to see. We are energy, and, as with all other forms of energy, we are invisible. Not only are we invisible, but also, as science will tell you, as energy we are indestructible, a concept that aligns with immortality!

The energy component of humanity has no physical properties at all; it is an elusive will-of-the-wisp. You can describe anything that has a physical component, but you cannot describe anything that has no form or substance detectable by the physical senses. Try describing sound to a person who has been deaf since birth!

Any material object can be described and illustrated, for it has color, weight and shape. These components are necessary for anything to be defined as a physical object, or matter. Look around you. Every object that you can see has all three components. Energy comes in many forms or guises, some crude and some sublimely pure, but the overriding fact is that you cannot see it. It has no physical component, no matter what its guise or form: *its presence can only be detected by the effects it creates*. No dictionaries that I have seen actually define what it is; they all refer to what it does. That is perfectly understandable, for energy has no weight, no color and no form – all negatives – but it can create effects, hence this Causism definition:

> Energy has no substance, no weight, no color, and no form. It does produce effects.

The *human energy unit* is the purest form of energy in this universe. It is the energy that is basic to the entire universe, and is not only indestructible (immortal), but is alone in its ability to store knowledge at a conscious level. Its invisibility is the source of the lack of understanding of human emotions, for all human emotions are the results of invisible energy fields impinging on the body.

Connecting human nature and energy

To have a full grasp of our true nature, it is necessary to understand something of the nature of energy, for within that concept lies the secret of our existence. This, in turn, is the key to understanding not only why we behave as we do, but also, as already stated, how we are now able to change our lives for the better.

If you ask an atheist whether they accept the existence of magnetism, they will invariably say 'Of course', and will probably look at you with an air of condescending tolerance. Ask them if they accept the existence of gravity, electricity or steam, and the response will be similar.

Now ask if they can see magnetism. Many will ignore the preciseness of the question and say you can see magnetism by the way it attracts other metals, metal filings or pins for example. The conversation will probably go something like this.

'Do you know much about magnetism?'

'A fair bit.'

'Can you see magnetism?'

'Of course you can!'

'Are you sure?'

'Of course I am! Every kid who did experiments at

school with magnets, pins and metal filings etc. has seen magnetism!

'Okay. I understand your answer, but the question was, "Can you *see* magnetism?" Seeing magnetism is one thing, but seeing its effects is another.'

'See it? Oh... I suppose not. But you certainly know it's there.'

If you hold a pencil out from your body and let it go, it will drop onto whatever is below it. As with magnetism, it is the effects of gravity that are visible, not gravity itself.

What this action plus the above conversation illustrate is that the existence of any form of energy is only apparent by the effects it creates, and one of those effects is human emotion. A bit left field, but true nevertheless.

The Steam Age demonstrated the benefits of harnessing the energy inherent in steam, yet you cannot see it – vapor yes, but not steam. The energy known as steam is invisible – it is transparent and colorless. Many people mistakenly think that what they see coming out of a boiling kettle is steam, but it is water vapor created by the steam contacting the cooler atmosphere. It is only when the vaporization occurs, when steam comes into contact with the air, that one is aware of the presence of steam – but you see the vapor, not the steam. Once again, you only know it is there by the effect it has created.

Electricity is another valuable form of energy, the

harnessing of which has provided countless benefits. To harness electricity effectively you need a conductor for it to travel along and to enable it to be insulated and controlled. Once again, you cannot see the energy called electricity; you can only observe its effects, for good or bad. When you see lightning, which is only an enormous spark, you are seeing a phenomenon created by electricity, not electricity itself.

As valuable as electricity is in our present society, it is a relatively crude form of energy when compared with magnetism Not as crude as steam, for example, but still relatively crude. Electricity can be insulated by a material such as rubber, and also requires a conductor, whereas magnetism is a highly refined form of energy that does not require a conductor. The same rubber that insulates electricity is no barrier to magnetism. If you do not have subjective reality on this, put a magnet on one side of a piece of rubber and a pin on the other side, directly opposite the magnet. The pin will remain in place. Naturally enough, the strength of the magnet, the thickness of the rubber, and the weight of the object have to be taken into consideration. A magnet, a piece of glass and a steel ball bearing will produce the same result. As you move the magnet, the ball bearing will follow on the other side of the glass. Even the various bits of information and photographs that are held on the household refrigerator attest to the nature of magnetism.

One of the limitations of magnetism is that it will only affect ferrous metals; it can only attract or repel such metals. Copper, for example, is immune to the effects of magnetism. Another limitation of magnetism is that it can be overridden by gravity, except when concentrated locally.

Gravity is demonstratively a far more potent form of energy, for there is no material object on this planet immune to the effects of gravity. Every minute speck of matter is on or in our planet simply because of the existence and strength of gravity.

Different forms of energy vary in effectiveness, and it is their effectiveness that classifies them. Take steam, electricity and even gravity for examples. Gravity is an integral component of this planet. It is also an integral component of our solar system, for it is the pushing and pulling of gravitational forces between and within the bodies of our solar system that keep it in balance.

A magnet can, to some degree, overcome the force of gravity of the planet. It can, for example, hold an object in suspension so that the object does not fall. In the same manner, planet Earth can, to some degree, overcome the forces of gravity that bind our solar system. Likewise, the solar system can, to a degree, overcome the gravitational pull and push of the physical universe as a whole.

To give you more understanding of this, if you do not have that reality already, go outside one clear night and inspect the sky – the universe around us. The force holding in place the myriad objects twinkling there is the same force that holds our solar system together.

That energy, known as gravity, is a factor common to the entire physical universe, which it pervades.

Accepting the fact that all the celestial bodies in the physical universe are moving in relation to one another is simply accepting the fact that the forces of gravitational energy are still in the process of trying to find a balance. It is like putting a heap of iron filings in a magnetic field: they will move around until equilibrium is established. The same thing occurs when a magnetic compass is disturbed: the needle will swing back and forth until it settles again, pointing to the magnetic North. How long it takes to resume its northerly aspect is dependent on the inertia of the needle and the strength of the magnetic field. Similarly, how fast the iron filings move and how long they take to settle around a magnet are entirely dependent on the same factors. The movement within and between the galaxies in the universe is the same thing on a larger scale, and the greater the distances, and the greater the mass in motion, the greater the *time* necessary to find equilibrium.

An object without its own energy source is said to be inanimate, meaning it requires an outside source of energy if it is to change its position. This is demonstratively apparent in the case of a stone lying on the ground. That stone, a part of the physical universe, will never change its position in relation to its surroundings unless some energy is applied to it. This is true of any inanimate object. No matter how expansively you extrapolate the concept, a material object will not move without some form of energy being applied to it. Isaac Newton did extensive research in this area.

Two logical questions now arise: 'Where does the physical universe come from?' and 'Where does energy come from?' Scientists are currently debating the Big Bang theory in an attempt to answer the first question, but it is the second question that must be answered in order to address the first.

Let us have another look at magnetism and its relationship to electricity. Although electricity can be created chemically, such as in a simple battery, it has only become a commercial proposition because a generator can create it mechanically. An electric generator has a ferrous metal core around which is wound non-ferrous material – copper wire. This is then rotated mechanically in a magnetic field, in other words between magnets. It is the movement of the copper wire within the magnetic field that creates the electric flow within the wire, for it is the changing position of the magnetic field in relation to the wire that causes the generation of electricity. A stationary wire with a magnetic field passing over it will have the same effect.

Conversely, ferrous metal can be induced with a magnetic field by applying electricity to it, so you can see that both electricity and magnetism go hand in hand, but each is dependent on the other.

If you look into this a little more deeply, revolving the copper wire requires harnessing some other form of energy – a steam engine, a diesel engine or even a human body. You are not really creating energy, but simply changing it into a more manageable form. Even if you create electricity by harnessing the power of falling water (hydro-electricity), you are simply harnessing the power of gravity and turning it into another form of energy. *You cannot destroy energy; you can only change its class or type.*

These examples illustrate that energy is an inherent component of the physical universe, and that science and industry do not *create* energy – they simply change it into a more manageable form. Energy cannot be destroyed, but its form can be changed.

All living organisms, be they inhabitants of the animal world or the immobile plant world, are activated by a form of energy. All organisms follow the principles of birth, development (maturing) and finally death. No organism, mobile or immobile, is an exception. It is the effectiveness of different forms of energy that separates life forms. The supreme energy form of the universe activates humans, and it is this fact that separates us from all other forms of life. The closest energy to our own class, the human spirit, is apparently the class of energy activating primates.

These data necessitate a re-examination of the concept of evolution. It is not the genetic structure that separates us from primates, but the form of energy that activates the genetic structure. Genetic structures may be subject to evolution, but not the energy that activates them.

We have illustrated that it is only the effects of

energy – the manifestations of energy – that are visible. Exactly the same principle applies in establishing the presence of the human energy unit. We have also established the fact that an object will not move until or unless an energy form is applied to it. The human body is no different: it will not and cannot move without some energy being present to activate it. The movements of the human body are the manifestations of an energy force being present, and that energy force is obviously within or around the body.

The human body is mobile and functioning only when it is controlled by a resident energy form. Death is simply the energy departing, at which time the body becomes just another material object. At this stage, some thinking individual will state that it is the food we eat that provides the energy for the body. Perfectly true, but there are two factors involved: the driving force that motivates the body, and the bodily energy required for it to function as a separate entity. The body converts the food we eat into energy, just as fire converts combustible material into heat and light, but as just stated, it is the *human energy unit* that is the prime mover.

To return to the principle that energy is only recognizable by the effects it creates: it is obvious that every movement of a human body is a manifestation of an energy unit operating independently of an outside source. The real you is not a body; you are an energy unit inhabiting a body. An enormous hurdle is surmounted the moment you accept the fact that you are a class of energy, albeit invisible and undetectable by human senses. This energy unit, just like gravity, cannot be insulated by matter; and just as magnetism and gravity can permeate matter, so too can the human spirit. How else can a person feel that they are within their body? If they can get into a body, they must also be able to get out, hence the numerous stories of 'out-of-body' experiences. Both these phenomena are readily understood when the human energy unit's ability to permeate matter is accepted. As will be explained in the next chapter, most energy forms have an effect on material objects, but the human energy unit is so pure it just passes through matter. The X-ray has a degree of this ability in that it can pass through human tissue but not through bone.

A spiritual being fully meets the definition of energy, for that is what it is – pure energy. It has however, an added ability that makes it the supreme form of energy: it is able to store knowledge and think. In other words, it is able to compute, rationalize and make decisions.

The quality of energy

There is no such thing as poor-quality energy, be it electricity, steam, gravity or magnetism. The strength may vary, but not its inherent nature. Energy is what it is: perfect in its own right, no matter what its class. Therefore the human energy unit must also perfect! This begs the question, 'If we are perfect, how is it that life itself is not perfect, for individuals, or humanity as a whole?' The magnitude and the importance of that question are beyond calculation. It was one of the first questions I asked myself – and it has at last been answered.

CHAPTER 6

Science, humanities and Causism

Today, the material sciences have broken technical barriers that would have had people from the nineteenth century gasping in disbelief. The speed of evolution in the material sciences even leaves today's elderly struggling to cope with the changes in their lives, so rapid is scientific advancement.

A little over 100 years ago, humans were not even flying in heavier than air machines, yet today individual planes are flying with hundreds of passengers and some exceed the speed of sound. We have even left the confines of Earth's gravity, and have people working in platforms in space. In a little over 100 years, we have progressed from the first wireless communication to the computer, television, satellite navigation and guided missiles with their frightening accuracy and power. The awesome power of the first atomic bomb has been the subject of history lessons in our schools for decades.

Along with these advances, the medical world has made tremendous strides in the care of our bodies, prolonging useful life-spans with X-rays, ultrasound, keyhole surgery and organ transplants, to name but a few.

What about the humanities – the intangible social aspects of life such as literature, philosophies and an understanding of our true selves, as distinct from the tangible physical environment and our bodies? How far has our understanding of ourselves as sentient beings advanced? This question may seem rhetorical, but it is not, for the material sciences have left the humanities far in their wake, and the situation needs to be addressed.

Across the international panorama, despite the myriad scientific achievements, religious and racial intolerance is still fomenting devastating wars. The incredible inhumanity of these conflicts is daily fare on our television screens. Our newspapers are also filled with turbulent marriage breakdowns, horrendous crimes and incredible anti-social behaviors, which are accepted as the norm in today's society. Stress, depression, compulsive behavior and addictions to various substances are also an accepted part of life. Unfortunately, so too are the chemical compounds that are being increasingly prescribed for these personal maladies, for they are being spewed out in an endless and horrifically expensive stream. In coping with trauma and stress in the short term, sedatives and, to a lesser extent, anti-depressants are valuable commodities, but when they become the only and permanent solution, that is another matter entirely. We put men on the moon many years ago, but the search for a cure for depression, for example, has been largely abandoned and replaced with behavioral regimens to cope with its manifestations. Failing that, drugs are resorted to, both medicinal and off the street, but in both cases depression's manifestations are being addressed, rather than its causes. Even children are being prescribed drugs for perceived emotional problems!

Despite millions of hours of research and work by countless dedicated individuals in the emotional healing field, the reality is that conventional teachings do not provide the answers to emotional problems – hence the proliferation of drug-based solutions.

In the light of treating manifestations rather than causes, the alternative health industry is flourishing. The very proliferation of alternative counseling practices is testament to this. Unfortunately, even these practices are largely only addressing the manifestations and not the causes.

Wisdom is inherently aligned to an understanding of ourselves, of humankind as a whole, which automatically separates it from the scientific knowledge of the material sciences. So what has happened to

117

the humanities? What has happened to the goal of wisdom, the goal of a true understanding of us?

Somewhere along the line, the humanities have been derailed. There are reports that in some universities philosophy has disappeared from the curriculum, and in newer universities it has never even appeared. Yet the word philosophy means love of knowledge, love of wisdom – the very pursuit for which universities were originally founded.

In today's society, happiness is pursued via the accumulation of material wealth. The mad scramble to achieve it is generally paramount over any and all other considerations. Ironically, the only happiness anyone ever finds comes from within. Today, only in the field of religion is the human spirit afforded any great importance. But the answers do not lie in religious practices either – the answers lie in a deeper understanding of the human psyche, devoid of religious connotations. It is arguable that because the spiritual component of humankind has generally been assigned as the province of religion, any genuine scientific study of this spiritual component appears to be non-existent. Tragically, by aligning spirituality with religion, any attempt to discard religion brings with it the shunning of spiritual values and, at worst, the doctrine of atheism.

As I am not trained in the discipline of psychology, I am free from the strictures of its conventional ideas and teachings. This has allowed me to have a completely unbiased approach to the subject of human behavior, borne from a deep-seated love of knowledge. Philosophy as 'love of knowledge' is where my expertise lies as a humanist. Psychology currently deals with human behavior and not, as its name implies, with the study of the human psyche. It is an odd twist that although lacking any formal training in that discipline, my research has drifted into the very area from which psychology originally derived its name. According to *The World Book Dictionary*, its origins are: *psyche*: the human spirit; *ology*: a branch of knowledge. Therefore the meaning of psychology is 'a study and knowledge of the human psyche'. Resolving emotional problems was not the original intent of my research; it was aimed at developing human potential. But, with hindsight, the two are inescapably connected.

Added to this deep-seated love of knowledge is perseverance, the same credential enjoyed by Marconi. Marconi failed his entrance examination to university, but despite his lack of tertiary education, he is, as a result of persevering with his ideas, acclaimed today for his work in developing wireless communication. Perseverance was also the hallmark of many other historical figures remembered for their work in areas in which they had no formal training, people such as Harrison, the carpenter who developed the chronometer; the illiterate barber Ark Wright, who perfected the spinning machine; and Watt, who created the first practical steam engine, yet started life as an apprentice instrument maker.

Fortunately, the ability to read, a thirst for

knowledge, and a deep and abiding interest in the spiritual component of humankind – shorn of any religious considerations – have stood me in good stead. To parody Descartes, 'I am, therefore I can think and reason.' My interest goes back nearly 50 years, when the incidents described in Chapter 11 occurred. Other psychic experiences, some related and others not, consolidated the newfound awareness of my true nature. Since 1984, having failed to find the answers to my questions in the works and writings of others, I have been engaged in full-time independent research into the true nature of our existence.

In life you can become a wrecker or a builder. The easy option is the former. In the same vein, it is easy to criticize but not so easy to have a constructive solution. One of the standards by which I live is never to criticize unless you have a solution. Much of the above could be said to be critical, but in line with my own creed, any criticism is made after having produced a constructive answer. Years of research, experimentation and philosophizing have produced a totally new understanding of life, a totally new body of knowledge, called Causism (see Chapter 4).

Causism has created an entirely new paradigm in the field of personal development, health and well-being, a paradigm of vast proportions and significance in improving inter-personal relationships. Not only is it a quantum leap in an understanding of life, but its unbelievably simple method to alleviate emotional suffering has put the humanities back on the rails, and truly brought them into the twenty-first century alongside the material sciences.

After years of refinement, the procedures remain simple. They permanently and rapidly erase all negative emotions, and in doing so restore a person's sense of well-being and self-worth. The real you emerging is self-empowering, for the procedures do indeed enlighten people as to their true nature and potential.

The principle underlying the procedures is to remove accumulated negative alter egos, thereby exposing the true self. The more of these negative alter egos that are dis-created, the more there is of *the real you*, and the more you are in control of your own life, hence the mission statement, 'To assist people to be in control of their lives and live their own dreams.' The choice of the word 'own' in relation to dreams may sound superfluous. You think your dreams are your own, but not necessarily so, for many people are, for example, saddled with the dreams of their parents. I once knew a bank manager who took up that profession because of parental pressure, but all he ever wanted to do was be a train driver! This may sound like some childhood fantasy, but when a man in his fifties still talks about that fantasy with a sense of nostalgia, it goes deeper than that, even if it was held while still in the glamour and mystique of a predominantly steam age.

I am living my own dream, epitomized in the mission statement, and this is why I derive so much satisfaction from clients who tell me that they are now in control of their own lives. The following is an excerpt from a typical unsolicited e-mail from a person in another city, who was helped over the phone. Formerly suicidal, her words speak for themselves. There are many similar testimonials on file.

> ...The other developments are also interesting. I'm still testing out my 'new skin', as it were. I feel quite different and it's still hard to describe.
>
> It's as if I have fewer limitations all of a sudden. Missing is the sense of despair and foreboding – I no longer wake with the feeling that I want to 'end it all'.
>
> The benefits of this change are huge. I'm able to focus on the practical aspects of my life without anxiety and fear, and don't see every obstacle as insurmountable, as I did before.
>
> I have 'courage', something I've not had in a long, long time. There had been aspects of my life I previously avoided addressing because they caused so much pain. To be able to look at these issues dispassionately and begin dealing with them is an empowering feeling. I'm stunned that 2 half-hour sessions have had so much impact!

Unfortunately, the healing profession has historically had to be dragged kicking and screaming into any new paradigm. Two examples of this are described in detail in Chapter 11, both of which, ironically, are well known in the medical profession. On the fortunate side, an expanding number of qualified practitioners and trainers are operating not only in Australia but also in America, Canada, New Zealand, Singapore, England and other countries in Europe.

PART 3

Applying the Mace Energy Method

CHAPTER 7

Dis-creating negative identities

The key to the Mace Energy Method lies in locating the negative identities that are adversely affecting your emotional (and possibly physical) health and your interactions and relationships with others. Once identified, these negative identities can then be dis-created by the simple procedures outlined in this chapter.

Very importantly, and unlike most forms of counseling and similar methods of 'emotional healing', the Mace Energy Method is entirely devoid of self-disclosure. There is no need for the practitioner to know any of the details of the upsets that led to the negative identities being created, and therefore no need for you to have to re-call and re-live any distressing events that may have occurred. This aspect has proved to be of enormous relief to many people, not least for those who have experienced rape or other seriously emotionally disturbing events in their lives. One of the practitioners I trained some years ago recently related to me an incident involving a young woman who had sought his help after having been raped. On hearing that she did not need to go through the details of her dreadful ordeal again, she burst into tears of relief and explained that she had already seen several 'conventional' counselors, to each of whom she had had to describe – and re-live – her traumatic experience.

For optimal results, it is best to consult a trained practitioner. However, although it is not possible to dis-create your own negative identities – for the reasons explained later in this chapter ('The self-help concept') – it is possible to perform the Mace Energy Method to some effect with a friend, providing he or she also understands the underlying principles and the practical applications as outlined in the various chapters of this book.

Below is a transcript of an actual session. It describes the procedure that has been successfully carried out on many occasions, not only by me but also by those who have been trained in one of the academies. It is no longer theory, but proven reality.

Exclamation marks punctuate important practitioner statements to indicate that they are instructions rather than polite requests. Unvoiced, but necessary, explanations for the benefit of readers are in italics. During the conversation, some important data already given in earlier chapters will be repeated, but it is included here just as it is explained to a new client unfamiliar with the procedure.

******

Practitioner: It is generally accepted that we humans are composed of three elements, mind, body and spirit; but a remarkable discovery has been made. There is a fourth element, which has been called an identity. An identity is like an alter ego, or another self, a substitute you. We all have numerous identities, some with a negative content, and some with a positive content. Together they form your personality. But it is the negative ones we are interested in, because they contain all the negative aspects of your life. They are the source of depression, unwanted feelings, phobias, compulsive behavior, low self-esteem and all negative thoughts about you – in fact, anything about your own personality or make-up you do not like or would like to change. These negative identities are really invisible energy ridges around you, which usurp your basic personality and impose their own negativities on you. By basic personality, I mean *the real you*.

The negative identities are so much a part and parcel of your life that you erroneously think they are you. But they are not; they are something you have unknowingly created during moments of emotional stress, in other words *upsets* … and each upset contains two of them. The very fact that these identities seem so much a part of you makes it impossible to locate them intellectually. No matter how long you spend talking about your emotional problems, no matter how much introspection you engage in concerning them, you will never locate the relative negative identities that create these problems. They are too subtle and too deeply buried in the psyche to be located in that manner. This is a major difference separating us from counseling: we have realized the futility of talking about your problems; in fact, talking about them can often make them seem worse.

An upset is simply anything that has happened to you that you did not enjoy. It always has unwanted feelings. We do not categories or class upsets, because there is no interest in what happened. An upset is an upset is an upset! It is any event that adversely affected you.

Fortunately, because the negative identities have their source in an upset, we can locate them via an upset and tap into their negativities. It is akin to sneaking in the back entrance rather than coming in the front door. It is important to know that the nature of the upset does not matter; what happened in the upset does not matter; when the upset happened does not matter; whether you were 2 or 22 at the time of the upset does not matter; and whether it happened yesterday or 10 years ago does not matter. Nor does it matter how long the upset lasted, whether it was minutes, hours or weeks. Who else was involved in the upset does not matter. We are only interested in *you* and how *you* felt during the upset, so we do not need to know anything about the upset except *how it made you feel* and, to a minor degree, where it happened so as to orient you into it and extract the vital data.

(*The repeated use of the word upset is not particularly good grammar, but it is deliberate, to make sure an upset is triggered.*)

While I have been talking about upsets, your attention will have gone to some upset you experienced in the past; as I just explained, when it occurred does not matter and how long it lasted does not matter. From all the upsets you have experienced, your attention has homed in on one particular upset! Why? Because deep down, intuitively, you know it contains the two most negative elements in your life … the two most negative and unwanted aspects of your whole life. *Deep down you know.* Whether the upset seems major or minor is unimportant. That is the upset we are going to use. A minor upset is like the acorn, which produces the mighty oak tree; it is amazing what seemingly minor upsets harbor.

I will now explain to you the connection between negative identities and the upsets that are their source. In every upset there is an unwanted feeling. It is the feeling that matters, not what caused it. Because you did not like it, you resisted it, and *what you resist persists*. The feeling sits there, buried in your psyche, and becomes a negative identity, waiting to be triggered.

Client: But why does it persist?

Practitioner: Okay. Here is an example. Resist thinking about it!

Client (a little puzzled): Thinking about what?

Practitioner: A tiger. Resist thinking about a tiger! (*Pause*) You have pictured a tiger haven't you?

Client: Yes, but...?

Practitioner: Okay. I do not mind you asking questions. I want you to ask them if you do not understand something. But I want to ask you this: have you ever been in trouble for asking too many questions?

Client: Yes. When I asked Mum where babies came from.

Practitioner: Okay. We will handle that later if necessary. But what happened to the image of the tiger?

Client: It went, but it's back again!

Practitioner: It went because when I put your attention onto something else, you ceased resisting it! It has come back because I put your attention on it again.

Client: Hm, interesting.

Practitioner: The point is that you have to *create* something to be able to resist it; otherwise you would not know what it was you had to resist. Stupid I know, but that is how it is. When the unwanted feeling hits you, you resist it and set up a continuum, a continuous cycle of resist, create, resist, create... That feeling, like the image of the tiger, will sit there buried in your psyche until you cease to resist it, and only then will it disappear. This is what my method achieves: it

131

takes away the 'resist' and then the feeling disappears permanently. But in the meantime, the feeling just sits there and becomes a negative identity buried in your psyche, just waiting to be triggered, which is rather frequently.

Client: That certainly makes sense.

Practitioner: Good. But that is only part of the story. Every action is preceded by a decision, and what is not generally realized is that all people make a stream of decisions during every waking moment of the day and, importantly, each and every decision is aimed at their own survival. Some decisions are mundane and some more profound. For example, feeling hungry produces the decision to eat, and feeling thirsty produces the decision to drink; but on a more negative plain, before someone robs a bank he or she has to decide to do so. On a personal plain, you are sitting in that chair because you decided that maybe I could help you – a pro-survival decision, probably made after some reflection.

The paramount urge in life is personal survival, and when something happens that upsets you (threatens your survival), the urge to survive kicks in, causing you automatically to make a decision to handle it. Unlike the considered decision to consult me, the pro-survival decision in an upset is vastly different; it is purely an un-thinking, knee-jerk reaction made without any rational thought whatsoever. A practical analogy is if your hand accidentally touches something very hot. Do you leave your hand there while you decide what to do about it? Of course not! You remove it instantly without the slightest thought. An upset is no different: you react immediately. You automatically make a decision to sort the upset out, to explain to yourself why it happened; it is an instantaneous decision, an unthinking, knee-jerk reaction, made without any consideration of future consequences. For instance, to help explain this, if the hand feeling the heat is holding a cup full of liquid, some of the liquid will no doubt be spilt as the result of the sudden movement of the hand. Maybe it's a mundane example, but all threatening situations have the same mechanics: the reaction to the perceived threat produces its own unwanted consequences, as I will now explain.

Whenever a person makes a decision it always mirrors their mood level. Happy people make happy decisions. Sad people make sad decisions. A sad person has never, ever made a happy decision! More than that, because at the moment of upset your attention instinctively goes onto you, whatever the decision is, it will be about you as a person – you turn on yourself! If you are feeling upset about something, your attention is on you, on the effect it is having on you.

It is very important to understand this, for this is the source of all negative thoughts and feelings about yourself, such as feeling inferior and incapable – not that I am implying you feel that way. Once you have made that decision, it gets buried in your psyche and sits there from then on as a hypnotic command, to be continually dramatized. It becomes *the bane of your life*.

Okay! Any questions? No? Good! We will start. Close your eyes please and keep them closed unless I ask you to open them. Now this upset, which got triggered and which you now have your attention on, where did it occur? At home! At school! At work! Where?

Client: At home.

Practitioner: Okay. Now go to the very worst moment in that upset! You are now in the worst moment. Stay in that worst moment! In this worst moment it is as if you are in suspended animation. Nothing is happening, it is as if you are watching a stuck TV picture or you have pressed the pause button on a video! You are frozen in time! Nothing is happening or being said. Stay there! Exactly where are you frozen? Sitting? Standing? Lying down? Which?

Client: I'm standing in my cot.

Practitioner: Okay! Now stay standing there in that worst moment. An unwanted feeling has overwhelmed you! What is this unwanted feeling?

Client: Feeling rejected. This is amazing. If you had asked me when we started what troubled me the most I would never have given you that, but I realize now how true that is. Mum and Dad walked out and left me without saying a word.

Practitioner: You are only affected by what you do not know about! If a client tells me that they know what their problem is, I know with absolute certainty that is not their real problem!

(*The client had started talking about the incident, explaining it, so he was no longer in the worst moment.*)

Practitioner: Okay! Go back to that worst moment! Now stay in that worst moment! I want to check that we have the major feeling. Stay in that worst moment! Does this feeling of being rejected permeate the whole upset?

Client: Yes.

Practitioner: Now, because it is unwanted you are resisting it, and what is resisted persists. It sits there buried in your psyche, a negative feeling or attitude that is the bane of your life! Is that true?

Client: It's the story of my life!

Practitioner: All right. Now stay in that worst moment! You are standing there, overwhelmed by this feeling of being rejected! You have turned on yourself and made a negative irrational decision about you as a person! It is like a conclusion you have arrived at to explain your predicament! It's a knee-jerk reaction! It is not true! It's rubbish! But what have you decided about you as a person? I am what?

Client: I am unlovable.

Practitioner: Great. You are handling this extremely well. Now from what you have just told me, I suggest that what we have uncovered, feeling unlovable and feeling rejected, are the banes of your life. You know they are both irrational, but they continually rear their head and you have to fight them off. You know they are irrational, but it does not make them go away. They

135

just sit there. Is that true?

Client: As I said, the story of my life.

Practitioner: Okay. You were told at the start that the upset that got triggered held the two most negative aspects of your life. That statement is real to you now isn't it! They are the two negative identities that have the most adverse effect on your entire life! They are referred to as your ruin! I need now to tell you about these identities. Importantly, the only power they have is what you give them, for they generate no power of their own. They can be likened to a car battery that is completely dependent on the car's charging unit for its own charge. As far as your identities are concerned, they are totally dependent on you to keep them charged and operational. Unfortunately, over time, they take control of you, for you invest too much power in them. Also, over time, they develop other negative traits, for each of them is really a package of negative traits, held in place by a single core trait, which predominates. Fortunately, this core trait is like a lynch pin, for when it goes, all the other traits go with it. In your case, the core items are *rejected* and *unloved*. They hold all the other numerous negative traits together.

The resolution and dis-creation of these negative identities rely on an amazing discovery concerning the mind. It has none of the powers and abilities attributed to it. Its only function is to create a mental image of what you have your attention on. It does not store knowledge, evaluate situations or make decisions. It is purely a stimulus–response mechanism. Close your eyes and I will demonstrate that for you. Carrot! What are you looking at?

Client: A carrot.

Practitioner: Okay. Motorcar! What color is it?

Client: A red Mercedes.

Practitioner: School!

Client: My old high school.

Practitioner: Okay! Open your eyes please. What this demonstrates is that the mind creates an image of whatever you have got your attention on, but *it has no other purpose*!

(*A pause to let that sink in.*)

That is only a part of the story, for the mind does have an incredible ability! It has the ability to create a mental image to represent an understood concept, and a concept, of course, is an idea or a notion about something. It is this ability of the mind that is harnessed in the method we are going to use. I will demonstrate that for you using two words, which are nouns. The first word is *love*. You cannot see or touch love; it is a concept. Close your eyes again and just think what love means to you! (*Pause*) Okay. You have an image don't you! What is it?

Client: My daughter.

Practitioner: Good. You obviously love your daughter very much! The image of her represents love for you. We will go to the other end of the scale now. Anger! Think what anger means to you! (*Pause*) Okay. What is the image this time?

Client: A shaking fist.

Practitioner: All right. Open your eyes. That shaking fist represents anger to you!

Client: Amazing!

Practitioner: As I said, it is this amazing ability of the mind to create images to represent concepts that is harnessed and utilized in this model. I want to remind you that you were not asked to talk about love or anger, but only to think what those words meant to you. Anger and love are both concepts, and so also are identities. When I get you to look at each of the identities we found, separately of course, your mind will do its thing and create images, but – and this is important – *your mind cannot think. It is a stimulus–response mechanism without any powers to rationalize!* The image it creates will be anything from a donut to a dinosaur! Anything from a frog to an ice cream! It will just willy-nilly throw up any old irrelevant image. I do not care what the image is, but the first image that comes to mind is the one we need.

For demonstration purposes, let's assume you get a picture of a ball. You will then be told to focus on the image of the ball. As you do this, the image will get bigger and bigger. There is no limit to how big it can get. Its eventual size will indicate just how much power the identity exerts over you. Importantly, you can see the image but you cannot see yourself because you are energy and naturally invisible. But you can *feel* happy, sad, powerful, weak, big or small. Because that identity controls you and looks rather big, you are going to *feel* small in comparison. After the image has stopped growing, as you continue to focus on it, it will get smaller and smaller and reduce to no bigger than a speck. It will eventually disappear completely. There is no particular time involved.

Have a look at this drawing (*next page*). The top circle represents the image at full size. Alongside it is a dot that represents you looking at it, but feeling much smaller than it. The lower arrows indicate the energy flow from the image (identity) to you, causing the image to collapse and you to feel bigger.

Client: You want me to make the image smaller, is that right?

Practitioner: I am glad you asked that, because that is exactly what you must *not* do! I had better explain. It is to do with the idea that what you resist persists. If you try to make it smaller, you are actually resisting the size it is and it will not diminish. It is very subtle I know, but you must just look at the image and accept that it is as big as it is. Absolutely no effort is required, and no effort should be used. Just tell me what you see when I ask you.

Client: I understand.

Practitioner: Any other questions?

Client: No.

Practitioner: Good! We will get rid of your *rejected* identity first. Close your eyes please! Now just think what the word 'rejected' means to you! You will get an image and as soon as you do tell me!

Client: I have an image. It's a waterfall.

Practitioner: Great. Focus on this image. Just focus on it and it will grow. When it stops growing, tell me.

Client: It has stopped.

(*The time taken varies, but 20 to 30 seconds is average.*)

Practitioner: All right. How big does it seem?

Client: Enormous.

Practitioner: Okay. How small does it make you feel?

Client: Very tiny.

Practitioner: Okay. We will reverse the roles. Continue to focus on the image. (*Long pause*) Is it getting bigger or smaller?

Client: Bigger.

Practitioner: Okay. Keep focusing. When it stops growing, tell me.

Client: It has stopped.

Practitioner: Good. Keep focusing. (*Long pause*) Is it bigger or smaller now?

ENERGY FLOW

IMAGE
YOU

BALL

Client: A little smaller.

Practitioner: Good. Continue to focus. If it stops getting smaller or disappears, tell me.

Client: It's gone.

Practitioner: Great! How big do you feel?

Client: Huge.

Practitioner: Feeling huge is the real you! You are of infinite potential! Now, if that image has gone, the identity it represents has gone! It is out of your universe! You have *dis-created* it. And if that image has gone out of your universe and you are feeling huge, who is in control – you or that identity?

Client: Me!

Practitioner: Open your eyes when you are ready. Good. You are now in control. But let me tell you something! You did it, not me! You got rid of that identity, not me! Look at the mission statement! What does it say?

Client (reading): To assist people to take control of their own lives and live their own dreams.

Practitioner: That's right! You are taking control of your own life! You have made a major step towards really taking control of your own life!

We will now repeat the exercise on the other identity, the unlovable one.

(*This is done as for the first identity.*)

Practitioner: I am now going to check this out. Close your eyes please. Go back to that upset standing in your cot! Go back to what was the worst moment! How do you feel now?

Client: I feel kind of detached from it. I do not feel anything really.

Practitioner: Great! Open your eyes please. Actually you did not have to answer; the smile on your face is sufficient. But this is very important! *You cannot change the past, but you can change how the past affects you now!* The rejected and unlovable identities are now out of your universe and, very importantly, *they will never, ever return! I can guarantee that because of the law of survival!* I will even give you a lifetime guarantee of that! Knowing that law, I know that no one will ever knowingly do anything that impedes their survival, their happiness! You now know about those identities, and all the adverse effects they have had on your life, so you will never create them again! Would you ever put your hand in a bucket of boiling water? Of course not: you know what the consequences would be. Likewise, you will never create those identities again because you know how they have affected you in the past!

Client: It seems too good to be true! It's too simple!

Practitioner: I know how you feel; that is the response of almost everyone who sits there in front of me! Yes it is simple. But to give it another perspective, can you think of a mechanical contrivance simpler than the wheel?

Client (after a few moments' thought): No.

Practitioner: Can you imagine civilization without the wheel?

Client: That is a new thought.

Practitioner: Precisely! Without the wheel we would not even have a wheelbarrow! The wheel gets its power from its simplicity. This methodology also gets its power and effectiveness from its simplicity. This research has tapped into the building blocks of life, the fundamental laws of existence!

(*There is very often a bit of discussion at this point.*)

Practitioner: So far so good. But that is only the first action. As you sit here now, are you aware of any other unwanted emotion of any kind whatsoever? If you are, we will get rid of it.

Client: I'm a bit anxious.

Practitioner: If you are feeling anxious, it comes from a negative identity, so we will handle it. Close your eyes and just think what anxious means to you! When you get an image let me know!

Client: I have a horse.

Practitioner: Okay. I know it seems ridiculous, but that is how the mind operates. Now, focus on the image and let it grow to its full size!

(*The same dis-creating procedure is followed until the client is free of any unwanted feelings and emotions and is totally in control of all the areas addressed.*)

Practitioner: There is nothing more that you want to handle, which is great, but that is only the surface stuff.

We are now going to change over to what is called *relationship repair*. To do that effectively, it is necessary to dig a bit deeper into your psyche, so I need to explain something to you. Throughout our lives we meet people, groups, organisations, circumstances and things that adversely affect us. The optimum thing to do is to brush the effect aside – but that's easier said than done. Far too often we resort to sweeping the experience under the carpet, but the effects sit there, unknowingly impinging on you. The degree that you are the effect of those experiences is the degree to which you are not in control of your life! Look at that mission statement again! When you walk out of here I want you to be fully in control of your life!

You are now going to be asked a question. Optimally, there is no answer, and that is the ultimate goal, but that only very rarely happens initially. The answer is going to be an instantaneous one, a snap answer, not a think-about-it one. Here is an example of what is meant. What are two twos?

Client: Four.

Practitioner: That is right, four! You did not have to think about it, did you? You just knew it. Here is another one: what is 93 x 45? There is no snap answer for that is there? Even if you were good at mental arithmetic, you would have to think about it! That is what is meant by the snap answer: you do not have to think about it, because you know the answer!

Before proceeding, I want to explain something else. We all have numerous identities, some positive and some negative, and we automatically activate the one that is pertinent to wherever our attention goes. You have already demonstrated that you love your daughter! You feel good when you think about her, don't you?

Client: Of course.

Practitioner: That is to be expected. But now think of someone who recently upset you. Your feelings have immediately changed haven't they?

Client: Yes.

Practitioner: That is because you immediately dropped into another identity. You see, we continually go from one identity to another, depending on where our attention goes, and each identity has unique feelings, attitudes and abilities.

Okay! Here is the question! In your entire life, who or what has most adversely affected you?

Client: My father, but I don't see much of him.

Practitioner: That is not an issue, but before proceeding, a little more education. We are not going to handle your father per se, but what he represents. He is only the catalyst that has located two of your negative identities. What type of person is your father?

Client: Irresponsible.

Practitioner: That tells me that, as well as your father you react to anybody who you consider to be irresponsible and probably don't get on very well with.

Client: A few have come to mind.

146

Practitioner: Then it is real to you that your attitude to irresponsible people does not create good relationships.

Client. Yes. It is now.

Practitioner: The reason for this is that you have a negative identity that reacts to irresponsibility from any source, and we need to get rid of it. So let's get on with it. Close your eyes again. Now put your attention on that identity of yours that reacts to irresponsibility and you will get an image.

Client (after a little reflection): A shark.

(Standard procedure is now followed to dis-create the identity, then…)

Practitioner: There is still another action: we need to rid your universe of anything to do with irresponsibility. So close your eyes again and think what the word 'irresponsible' means and when you get the image, tell me.

Client: A man.

(Standard procedure again follows, then…)

Practitioner: Now what is important is that your father is what he is and you cannot change him, **but you do not have to be the effect of him!** Your father is irresponsible. Think about him. How do you feel about him now?

Client: Strange to say, but its compassion.

Practitioner: That is to be expected, for you are now rational towards him. What you now feel comes from

you, whereas before, all your feelings were from a negative identity. As from this moment, your flows, or vibes, towards your father have changed and although you cannot knowingly change him, he will change towards you because you have changed towards him. You are now in control of that relationship and, whatever the situation, you will say or do things that are right for you – in other words, behave rationally.

Client: He was not a very good father, but I don't seem to care about that anymore. I feel sort of neutral. All the arguments seem so pointless now.

Practitioner: That is great. Now, one final thing about this: think about the irresponsible people you know or have known. You feel different towards them now, don't you?

Client: I cannot even find any!

Practitioner: That's because that negative aspect of your personality has gone. You accept them for what they are without being the effect of them. Rational thoughts are pro-survival, but negative thoughts are non-survival.

Client: Can I say something about this, or about Dad really?

Practitioner: Of course.

Client: I would not have believed this a few minutes ago, it's as if I really understand him for the first time. He had a rather hard life, bringing all of us up...

Practitioner: Handling that part of your life is only the start. I am going to ask the question, 'Who or what is adversely affecting you?' again and again until there is no answer, for having no answers is the optimum situation. But realize that 'who' relates to any individual, and 'what' refers to anything else.

(Later, after the question has drawn a blank.)

Practitioner: We are now going to do the final action, the final check before we end the session. It is to make sure that nothing has been missed. Close your eyes please. Okay. Scan your entire life and if anything negative turns up, let me know!

(Quite often, the client will find something, and in that event, here is the standard response.)

Practitioner: You have thought of something. Good. Has your attention gone to an incident or a particular person?

Client: An incident.

Practitioner: Okay. Where did this incident occur?

(There is no point in relating the actual handling again, except to say that in this case it was the standard upset handling, but if it had been a particular person, the relationship repair would have been used.)

Practitioner: Okay. Close your eyes again and once more scan your entire life. If your attention goes to anything else, let me know.

Client (after a few minutes' reflection): There is nothing. I feel good.

Practitioner: Has this told you anything?

Client: Nothing really, but I feel really calm and

peaceful.

Practitioner: Okay. Well what it tells me is that nothing in your past is now affecting you; you are free to get on with your life. Your past is wiped clean, a clean slate so to speak, so just get on with your life. There are no exercises for you to do; just enjoy the real you and get on with your life. Now read that mission statement again!

Client: Strange to say, I feel different about it compared to the last time I read it. Then, it did not seem so real, but now I know I am in control of my life and it feels great.

Practitioner: Okay. That is the end of the session.

Note. *Many clients do not have to come back again; when they leave, they are in control of their lives. An average session is about 60–90 minutes.*

The above transcript describes an average session, but innumerable questions must have arisen while reading it, so the obvious ones will be answered now. While the above exercise is fresh in your memory, here is something to consider before proceeding.

The first requirement in understanding the dis-creation of negative identities is to confirm that they are indeed not you, that they are separate from you, something you have acquired, albeit unknowingly – in other words, you need to be fully aware that they are not you.

To start with, look around the room and pick out five objects. Having done that, answer this: 'Are they you?' The answer is of course 'No,' because, as expounded in Buddhist philosophy, you cannot see yourself, therefore everything you see cannot be you. Apart from that, from a scientific point of view, you cannot see yourself because, like all other forms of energy, you are invisible. This is a simple but very important exercise, as simple as the procedures themselves, but the simplicity of the procedures belies their effectiveness.

You will have to read this paragraph before you do the next exercise, because it requires you to close your eyes to do it. With your eyes closed, think of a cat. Whether it is black, white or tabby does not matter, but you will have a mental picture, a mental image of it (a mental image, of course, because it is in your mind).

Now answer this: 'Who was looking at the cat?' The answer is of course 'Me.' This little exercise has two elements. First, you were not using your eyes to see the mental image of the cat: it was *you* looking at it, not your body! Maybe this will be teaching you how to suck eggs, so to speak, but that simple exercise is the easiest way there is to demonstrate who you really are. It was the *real you* looking at that cat, and that is the simplicity of it. That exercise is ridiculously simple, but if you had any resistance to doing it – if you had any trouble in doing it or some unwanted feeling was triggered, in fact anything except the simplicity of viewing your mental creation of a cat – you triggered a negative identity. If that was the case, what you experienced was the dramatization (acting out) of the negative identity that the exercise triggered. This exercise underlines the fact that we are invisible entities, with unlimited powers, able to think, rationalize, make decisions, store knowledge (for example what a cat looks like) and envisage without the need of eyes. This equates with omniscience and omnipotence, the infinite you.

The second element is that if you were looking at the cat, it cannot be you. The cat image was certainly not something you could touch physically, but just as certain is the fact that the image was not you. In Chapter 3 you were asked to think about the meaning of the concepts of love, hate and anger. You would have envisaged a mental image to represent each one of those concepts. Recognizing this is an essential step in understanding what follows.

Just as those three emotions were concepts, so too are any negative identities. *Every negative identity is a concept,* and provided you understand what they mean, your mind will create a mental image to represent each one. Each mental image appears to represent the relevant identity, but actually they all represent the energy in the identity, a subtle but very important difference.

In practice, clients are asked to close their eyes and keep them closed for the duration of the action. There are two reasons for this. The first is to obviate them having any of their attention on their surroundings, so that their complete attention is where it is required – on the procedure and themselves. Second, when they envisage the image, they are not using their eyes, and therefore it can only be they, an energy unit, that are viewing it. The nature of the image is irrelevant; however, asking what it is ensures that the client is still cooperating, and is actually doing the exercise. Once clients have the image that represents the identity, they will realize that they are separate from it, because they can see it! They will know they are not the image, so they are not the identity! They have symbolically disconnected from it. Although they are aware of this, they are still the effect of it, still controlled by it, but now that they are separate from it they will no longer keep it charged.

The self-help concept

The question arises, 'Can I do this on myself?' Unfortunately, the answer is in the negative. The procedures known as the Mace Energy Method are not a 'self-help' model. It would be the realization of a Utopian dream come true if that were the case. However, as mentioned at the start of this chapter, there is no practical reason to prevent anyone using the procedures to help someone else. (See Appendix 3, *Training and personal help*.)

Concerning self-help, these words from Leslie D. Weatherhead's book *Psychology and Life* say it all (Weatherhead, 1935).

> The difficulty of observing your own mental processes is that you cannot see yourself by yourself, for when you look at yourself, you use a bit of yourself to see

yourself; so therefore it is not the whole of yourself you see, is it?

An interesting analogy has surfaced. If you are sitting in a car, you can only view the interior, not the exterior. You need to get out of the car – become exterior to it – in order to view it fully. The same applies to an unwanted identity: the moment you put your attention on it, you are *in it*, and can only have an interior viewpoint, instead of the necessary exterior viewpoint, as is available when under the direction of a practitioner.

An identity will only appear as a mental picture – a pictorial representation – when it is fully viewed; in other words, when the concept is complete. This makes the dis-creation of negative identities foolproof, but it also means that it is not possible to dis-create them on your own, as described so eloquently in Leslie Weatherhead's book. The following anecdote further emphasizes the importance of being supported by a Mace Energy Method practitioner.

In June 2004, there was an avalanche of computer viruses, and my computer did not escape infection, even though protected by a top-quality program. The general problem of computer viruses is that it is only when the virus is in circulation that the companies creating anti-virus systems become aware of its existence. These companies are invariably very quick to create a solution that can be downloaded, but that, as with mine, is often after the event. Although I had upgraded my virus protection program, there was one set of viruses I could not eliminate, and the message on the screen remained to warn me that the computer was infected. Frustrating, to say the least!

I took my computer to a computer expert, who hooked it up to an anti-virus system via the Internet. This program, which was, of course, external to my computer, cleaned the virus out quite quickly. The technician said, 'The trouble you were having was because the virus had got into your own anti-virus program and *it cannot clean itself.'* Here, in the physical universe, is an example demonstrating that no one can dis-create their own negative identities – they need the assistance and guidance of an external influence to do so.

In light of the fact that Causism aligns computer technology with how we human beings operate in life, including aligning a virus with a negative identity, it is ironic that it is a computer infected with a virus that finally confirms our inability to dis-create our own negative identities.

Just to make sure the message is understood, here is another little exercise. Think about someone who recently upset you, or someone you do not particularly like. Now think of someone of whom you are very fond – perhaps a loving spouse or a child.

Your feelings will be very different between the two. This is because, in life, following our attention, we all flip from identity to identity, and you cannot be in two identities at the same time. No matter how quickly you flip from one identity to another, you cannot be in a self-help identity at the same time as you are thinking about an identity you want to eliminate. So you cannot therefore be simultaneously both 'practitioner' and 'client'. In other words, there is no way a person can dis-create his or her own negative identities.

Some questions answered

Based on experience, here are the most common questions asked, with their answers.

Question. If the identities make up a person's personality, then you end up changing their personality. Is that correct?

Answer. Yes. We are all spiritual beings, or, as I prefer to say, energy units, that are perfect in their own right. You are not your personality. Your personality is something that *you* possess. It is a composite of all your identities. This is why anything you do not like about your personality can be changed. It must be understood, though, that no matter how powerful is this technology, it cannot change anyone who does not want to change.

Question. What is the 'worst moment'? You make a big issue of it. Why? If someone does not know when the worst part was, how can they find it?

Answer. The 'worst moment' is defined as 'the moment in an upset when the person is overwhelmed by the event. It is the moment that they became the total effect of it.' It is impossible for a client precisely to locate the worst moment in an upset by pondering on it. The whole event is emotionally painful, whether it lasts for a minute or a month. The following case history will help explain this.

A lady in her fifties came to me for assistance in sorting out some marital problems and also deep depression. As soon I started to explain the ramifications of upsets, she burst into tears. What had been triggered was a painful loss during her teenage years. Although I tried to convince her that relating the experience had no therapeutic value, she insisted: 'you need to know all about it so you will understand how I feel. Attitudes were different in those days, as you will appreciate!' (She was referring to me being much older than her.) I eventually convinced her to stop pouring her heart out by saying, 'It is not that I am not interested in you; you would not be sitting here now if that was the case. I do understand how you feel, but talking about it is only making you feel worse, and is of no real help.'

It transpired that she had been raised in a strict religious family but as a teenager had become pregnant out of wedlock, and had an abortion. Bearing in mind her religious faith, her regret, shame and deep grief were understandable. When told 'Go to the worst moment', she was standing at a bus stop. A pregnancy and an abortion do not happen overnight; weeks and perhaps months are involved. The fact that the client found herself standing at a bus stop gives a dimension to the 'worst moment' that words cannot describe, at least none that I can find, except to say that it is only the being per se and not the client (the person) who knows when the worst moment occurred; logical thinking does not come into it.

What happened at the bus stop, I have no idea, and, in fact, I do not know whether that moment occurred before or after the abortion. But it is indicative of the fact that only the being knows when the worst moment occurred. Maybe her boyfriend said, 'Are you sure it is me?'

After the identity-handling procedure, the tears were still there, but not the raw emotion; the tears, coming through a smile, were tears of relief, and gradually the smile took over and the tears ceased. After a minute or two to allow her to experience her newfound composure, this followed.

'Okay. Think about that event now! How do you feel?'

'I just feel calm about it. I had an abortion!'

It was a plain statement of fact, uttered through the calmness she was radiating – no tears, no hint of regret, no hint of guilt, just a calm acceptance of what she had experienced. With the calmness was the tacit realization that you cannot undo what has happened, but you can certainly undo the adverse effects it created.

Several concepts come together in the 'worst moment'; so let us examine the words involved. The word 'worst' is best described as 'there is nothing as bad as it', but the word 'moment' is not so simple. A moment is a split second in time that is so small it cannot be measured. A nanosecond is defined as a billionth of a second, but a 'moment' is so small it has never been given a finite quantity and never will be given a valid quantity, as it is timeless! It belongs in the energy universe, which is devoid of time.

This is an example of the laws of the material and energy universes differing and, importantly, that you cannot understand the phenomena of one by using the laws of the other. Of paramount importance is that an energy-universe problem cannot be solved with material-universe logic and laws. All unwanted feelings and attitudes stem from negative identities that are composed of energy, so they all follow the dictates of the energy universe. All 'mental health' problems are of the energy universe and not of the material or physical universe, which is why any discussion of 'mental health' problems, no matter what its nature, is really of no therapeutic value.

When clients, with their eyes closed, have their attention on the upset and they are told (not asked) 'Go to the very worst moment!' that is where they are. As explained in Chapter 3, and in the 'attention follows attention' concept, they cannot help but be there. Importantly, however, as unbelievable as it may seem, *they have been transported to the energy universe where there is no time!* Do not confuse the being, the human energy unit, with the body! As there is no time in the energy universe, everything that happened in the upset is encapsulated as knowledge in that timeless space. It is all there *now*, so that the client is aware of both the feeling they resisted and the decision they made.

Interestingly, a trick taught to all trainees is that if the client starts talking about the incident, explaining what happened or why, they are no longer in the timeless 'worst moment', and they are no longer in the energy universe, because if there is activity, there has to be time. The client is simply told, 'Go back to the worst moment' (see transcript).

If you have any doubts about this, maybe you did not do the exercise on time in Chapter 4, in which case it is suggested that the exercise be revisited, even if only with the intention of 'proving' it is not correct.

Question. Why is it that when one identity goes there is such a resurgence of well being? After all, you have only eliminated one feeling.

Answer. A very important aspect of negative identities is that they are a package of negative personality traits, held together with the core item, which is addressed in the dis-creation exercise. In the transcript, they were *rejected* and *unlovable*.

Early in the research, it was thought necessary to list all the items in the trait, but that proved not to be the case. From the research notes, here is an actual list of traits given by one client that made up the package for a *useless identity*:

* Worthlessness
* A sense of failure
* Hopelessness
* Alienation
* Powerlessness
* Fear

* Fatigue

* Gives up easily

* Depressed

* Hacked down

* A loser

* Lost.

It was when this last item was given that the mental image appeared. The core trait was *feeling useless*. Each core trait is like a lynch pin, and just as a lynch pin is the key to keeping an arch in place, so too does the core trait keep the entire package together. When the core trait goes, so too does the entire identity, which is why the results are so dramatic and rapid.

Question. You say that every upset contains two negative identities. Why are there always two? Why are there not more than two?

Answer. That first question is like asking 'Why do we need a mother and a father?' The second question is like asking 'Why can't you have two fathers?' The simplistic answer is, because that is how it is! If you re-examine the 'Upset phenomena' drawings in Chapter 2, it shows the two elements in an upset causing a negative identity. Using material-universe logic, it is obvious there are only two. Early in the research it was thought there was only one – the *decision identity*.

Question. If finding 'upsets' is a necessary part of the procedure, how come you just asked for an 'unwanted feeling' in the second part of the handling? Why not every time, instead of using an upset?

Answer. The question is simple, but the answer is not so simple or short, for there are quite a few aspects to it. In an upset, the two identities uncovered seem so much a part of a person's personality that the person assumes they themselves are the identities. Their very subtlety makes them immune from detection by any intellectualizing on the part of the client. A common identity is, 'I am not good enough.' Experience has shown that not a single client has ever volunteered or even suggested that they are the victims of such a notion. As mentioned, it is so much a part of them that they keep looking elsewhere. It must be stressed that a being's omniscience does not mean that they are aware of what they know! Most of what a being knows is buried deep, beyond conscious recall. When a client is told 'Go to an upset!' the upset they go to be what is called their *ruin*, because it holds the two most negative elements in their life, the two elements that most adversely affect their survival and happiness.

The diagram on the next page contains four elements: the paramount survival urge; the all-knowing being (the client); attention on upsets; and, the central element, the ruin. This last element is the product of the other three working in unison, and its genus is the concept 'attention follows attention', for when talking about upsets, the client's attention automatically goes onto upsets, and the one they go to is the one that needs handling the most – their ruin. This is an intuitive knowingness on their part. To explain the sequence of events, consider this. When you read 'mother', where does your attention go? When you read 'football', where does your attention go? Similarly, if upsets are discussed, that is where a client's attention goes, and when all three elements at the corners work conjointly, the client's knowingness homes in on the upset, which deep down they know needs handling above any other – hence 'the ruin' tag. Handling the two identities in the ruin is a major reason why very few clients need further sessions.

THE RUIN

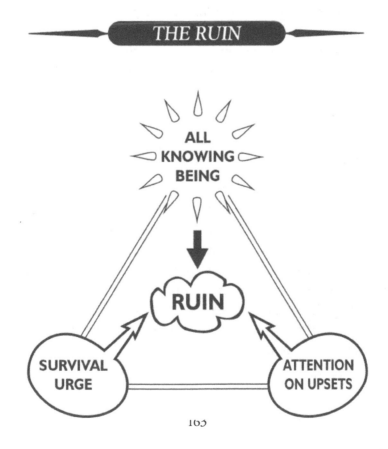

As in the transcript, after the two identities from the upset were eliminated, the client was asked if she was aware of any other unwanted feeling – referred to as a *residual feeling*. That is a legitimate way of locating identities, but the really insidious ones are the ones that sit there undetected and, as the client commented, the two from the upset were the story of her life. As often as not, there are no residual feelings, but the question is always asked as check.

Question. Why is it that *when* an upset occurred does not matter?

Answer. If a person is plagued by a 'useless' feeling, the identity causing it will have been triggered many times, in numerous upsets, so which upset a person goes to does not really matter, for it will always locate the relevant identity.

Question. If the identity gets triggered many times, causing many upsets, how many upsets, on average, have to be addressed?

Answer. Only one. Each upset is like a link in a chain: take out a link and the chain is broken. What link you remove does not matter. Every upset a person has ever experienced because of that particular identity now has no effect on them – the chain is broken. They can review each upset with equanimity. This explanation is a typical example of using material-universe logic to explain an energy-universe phenomenon: it sounds fine, but is not the real truth.

The real truth lies in the fact that there is no time

in the energy universe, and that it is energy causing the phenomenon. It was mentioned above that in the 'worst moment' there is no time, and that everything that happened in the upset is encapsulated in this timeless moment. It is from this timeless moment in the energy universe that the client is viewing the material universe, which is where the upset occurred.

Another thing to consider! The explanation of the upset phenomena in Chapter 2 entails a sequence of events, for it is using material-universe logic, which contains time. It started with the upsetting feeling and moved through various stages, so that it was the upset that was the root cause of everything that transpired, including the creation of the negative identities. Although it appears that way, it is not the actuality. In the energy universe, where all the effects came from, there is no time and therefore there can be no sequence of events. When viewed from energy-universe laws, there is only now – the whole incident occurred *now*! The whole event is in the same time frame! The ultimate conclusion is that the *identity* is the key element and not the upset. The proof of the pudding is in the eating. Once an identity has been dis-created, every upset involving that identity, no matter how many there were, is now just a memory and in many cases not even a memory. Even if the client remembers the events, the identities are no longer part of them, so they can recall them with equanimity and be totally non-affect, in the same manner that they could remember the mundane experience of having breakfast.

This circumstance is labeled the *chicken and egg* phenomenon, because just as both the chicken and the egg are dependent on each other for their individual existences, so also are the existences of both the upset and the identity totally dependent on each other.

There is a final twist in the saga of upsets and identities: the existence of a third universe. This is your own universe, composed of everything *of which you are aware.* 'Everything', of course, includes both energy and material. Your own universe has elements of the other two universes, therefore it can be said to straddle them, which is why the 'worst moment' is such a powerful instrument. In that moment, you are in the energy universe, from where you are viewing the material universe. Very important is the fact that a being in its native state, the energy universe, knows everything, and with your attention on the upset, you know everything about it, hence the recovery of all the details, including, of course, the unwanted feeling and the reactionary decision made.

To understand this fully, one has to be fully aware that there is no time in the energy universe – hence the reason for introducing the exercise on time earlier in the book.

CHICKEN AND THE EGG

BEFORE
SESSION

PAST UPSETS   **NOW**   **FUTURE UPSETS**

IDENTITY

AFTER
SESSION

NO IDENTITY

PAST UPSETS ONLY MEMORIES

NO FUTURE UPSETS

NO EFFECTS

Question. If the negative decision in an upset is non-survival, why is it made in the first place? Also, as it seems so easy to undo it, why is it not undone or countermanded straightaway, before it causes trouble?

Answer. The answer to the first part is that no one is blessed with foresight. Many decisions turn out to be anything but helpful, but at the time they were made they appeared to be helpful. If we were all blessed with foresight, no one would ever make a mistake! Once mistakes are made, they are buried out of sight, so to speak, hidden from the person who made them.

The other aspect goes much deeper and hinges on the difference between a person and a being. The being is an energy unit, which is omniscient and omnipotent, but the person is a composite of both the being and all its identities. The more negative identities that are present in the game of life, the more irrational decisions are made *by the person*, and the more mistakes are made. A fully aware being will never create anything that is non-survival, such as a negative identity.

The Mace Energy Method puts the being into the energy universe, where it is divorced from, and unencumbered by, its identities. Viewing them objectively from that position, the being, in recognizing their non-survival aspects, always dis-creates them.

Question. What makes the image change size when you focus on it?

Answer. Every identity is a package of traits, each with its own energy, and focusing on the image causes all the energy from the traits to come together, and this causes the image to get bigger. The image only stops growing when this has been done. The accumulated energy can now be recovered, which is why the client feels bigger and the image gets smaller. As for 'getting smaller', as mentioned in the previous answer, we are dealing with energy-universe phenomena and not material-universe phenomena, and neither is applicable in the other universe. Without going too deeply into this, in the energy universe there is an exchange of energy, which can be likened to telepathic communication, during which no physical communication or physical contact is necessary. The same applies to bleeding charge off a negative identity: no physical contact is necessary. This highlights a profound difference between the two universes.

In considering the broader application of the dis-creating process, I am reminded of Topsy, the intriguing young character in the novel *Uncle Tom's Cabin* who is credited as the catalyst for the American Civil War. If my memory serves me correctly, when asked when she was born, she replied, 'I was not born. I just grew!' Like Topsy, Causism just grew, and in the growing, a wide number of applications have been developed, but they all utilize the dis-creation of negative identities. The rationale of this is that we are all inherently perfect, and anything that detracts from that lofty infinite state must be an exterior force, and that exterior force is what Causism has called a negative identity.

Humans suffer many emotional ills, and no matter what they are, they all respond to the same simple basic procedure. Any difference lies in locating the unwanted identities that cause emotional disorder, no matter how they are labeled. Addictions, study problems, recurring nightmares, phobias, low self-esteem, chronic grief, post-traumatic stress disorder or post-natal depression – in fact, any emotional disorder you care to mention – all have their roots in negative identities. It is not an idle statement or a boast, for Causism ushers in a new age, a new paradigm in understanding human beings and the alleviation of emotional ills. In practice, various emotional conditions such as nightmares require a specialized approach to find the relevant negative identities.

Half a century of accumulated knowledge and experience gathered under the umbrella of Causism is offered for the price of this book, because of this credo:

> No individual, no group and no organisation, no matter how large and powerful, have a lien on knowledge. Knowledge belongs to all.

CHAPTER 8

Viewpoints

In the next chapter, we discuss the relationship repair action, but before doing so we should first consider the role that viewpoints play in all our relationships with other people.

From the moment of conception onwards, our environment moulds us. Our environment influences our individual view of life, to the extent that on almost every subject you care to choose, you will find people with differing viewpoints. People's life experiences, how their siblings, parents, schoolmates and teachers treated them, how they are treated in the work place, what they have read and what they have studied mould their viewpoints. Some people have loving parents, some have abusive parents, some are over-indulged and others deprived. Each individual views life in his or her own, unique manner, and responds differently in a unique manner, melded by the kaleidoscope of personal experience.

Every area of life produces different viewpoints, perhaps the best examples of which are the political and religious arenas. Therein, heated arguments are commonplace, with the antagonists forcefully expressing their own 'rightness', and invariably having no effect on the opinions of others. Politics and religion are behind most wars, both past and present.

We are all the product of our environment. If you talk to anyone with strong views about what they are doing, for example a social worker or a missionary, and ask what motivates them, or what influenced their choice of occupation, they will invariably relate certain experiences as having affected them greatly. These experiences were often deciding factors in their vocational decisions.

The frequently used expression 'Your attitude to life is colored by your experiences' is not only very true, but also very appropriate, and in fact was the genus of what follows.

As a hypothetical example, imagine four people wearing four different colors of tinted glasses to represent their experiences in life – one red, one green, one blue and one orange. There is a plaque on the wall and each person is asked its color. One sees it as red, one as blue, one as green and one as orange, and each *knows* he or she is right. Similarly, four people having a discussion about a particular subject may all have different and strongly held viewpoints, and each person may be convinced that he or she is right. Their experiences in life tell them they are right.

Therein lies the genus of every argument you have ever had: *you knew you were right!* Unfortunately, *the other person also knew they were right!* Each individual sees his or her own truth! If you can make this concept your own – in other words, accept the 'truth' of it for yourself, not just because of what you have just read – you will never again engage in the most fruitless of activities, arguing; debate maybe, but arguments never.

If people cannot accept the viewpoints expounded by others, the reason lies within their own negative identities. Accepting does not mean agreement; it simply means acknowledging to oneself that someone else sees things differently.

The quickest way to stop an argument is to say, 'You are right of course!' You will have some interesting responses! But by repeating, 'Yes, you are right of course,' all arguments will peter out, as your opponents will think you agree with them, that their viewpoint is the correct one, and there is nothing to argue about. All that your protagonists are doing is asserting that *they are right!* Of course, they are implying that you are wrong, but you know you are right so don't worry about it! Although this advice is given with tongue in cheek, it is the reality, for you have not changed your mind, any more than they have. Please note that I have

173

not suggested you add 'I am wrong', for that would be ridiculous. You, and the other person, are entitled to your own rightness!

That response may seem a little unreal, but simply ceasing to push your own viewpoint will result in the argument petering out. Duplicating the above is a major leap in understanding not only others, but also you and life in general.

Many years ago, whilst lecturing on the subject of viewpoints, I started with the phrase, 'The only truth is what is true for you.' In other words, 'If it is true for you, then that is the truth.' But further enlightenment has since shown me that although from a pragmatic point of view the phrase is correct, truth goes much deeper than that. This is easily demonstrated by having those four individuals remove their hypothetical glasses – to reveal that the plaque is white after all. They will certainly not argue now as to its color!

This raises a very important concept: 'Truth is what it is... not what you think it is,' or, as a friend of mine once said, '...not what you would like it to be.'

There is no doubt that everyone has a unique impression of everything they view, be it inanimate or animate, and that of course includes other people, and it is the view of others that is so pertinent in relationships. To elaborate on this, in a class of, for example, 30 children, each child has a unique view of the teacher. All the children will see some traits that are similar to what the others see, but no two children will see all the same traits. They may, for instance, all agree that the teacher is grumpy, but if each child were to describe the teacher truthfully, there would be some discrepancies in every case.

It is worthwhile examining this point from a materialistic aspect. The word 'viewpoint' means 'point from which to view'. If two people are sitting apart and a book is placed between them, with the cover facing one of them, the back of the book must be facing the other, so each must see the same book differently. One person can describe the back but not the front, and vice versa. Two different viewpoints of the same book! Put a third person to one side, and this person will have a third view of the same book. It is obvious that each sees the book differently; they have different viewpoints, because they are using different points from which to view the book.

The same applies, but to a lesser extent, if you line 20 people up in a row and put an object in front of them. The people on each end will have markedly different physical points of view when compared with each other, but people's viewpoints will gradually become more similar as we move towards the centre of the row. Very importantly, even the two people rubbing shoulders in the middle will have slightly different viewpoints, although it may appear that their viewpoints are the same.

It is impossible for two people, two objects, or two pieces of matter, to occupy the same space at the same moment in time. It is obvious that one has to move to make room for the other. They both exist, but in different places, occupying different spaces, in any one moment in time. This is material-universe logic in full cry.

What happens, however, if you apply energy-universe logic to the same circumstance, and replace the two people with their true selves, their invisible energy component, detached from a body, and then ask, 'Is it possible for the two of them to occupy simultaneously the same *point from which to view*?' On the face of it, the answer is 'Yes,' because there is no material component involved, but if that were to be achieved, a remarkable thing would happen.

Imagine two energy units viewing something from different positions, and then answer this question: 'How many viewpoints are there?' The answer is, of course, 'Two.' Now, remembering that energy takes up no space, have one of those energy units move towards the other and occupy exactly the same viewpoint. Now answer this question: 'How many points from which to view (viewpoints) are there?' There is only one answer: 'One viewpoint.' Two viewpoints have become one: one has disappeared as the second moved into its viewing point!

Once again, material-universe logic does not apply in the energy universe. In the energy universe there is no matter, therefore there is no impediment to occupying the same *point from which to view*.

From this flows a question: are they as one, or has one disappeared? Whether you consider that they are as one or that one has disappeared is the philosophical question you are left with, and I will not attempt to answer that question for you. However, I will add that from a pragmatic aspect the only truth is what is true for you, but is that the real truth? Whatever the answer, it puts a new complexion on affinity, and on the ultimate degree of affinity, namely *love*.

Love is an extremely high state of affinity! Affinity is defined as the attraction one has for another, and is even used in that context in chemistry. The degree that one loves another is the degree of affinity one feels for another. When two people are said to be 'in love', there is a desire for each to share with the other and to be as close as possible with the other. Each is strongly attracted by the other.

Affinity is an energy-universe phenomenon – not to be confused with sex, which is a material-universe phenomenon. The ultimate in sharing and being close is to occupy the same viewpoint, the same space; to be as one. This is what lovers do – they share their bodies.

The purpose of sex is not to create pleasure. Its purpose, no matter how pleasurable it can be, is the procreation of the species, driven by the paramount urge of survival. No matter what activities are carried out under the sexual drive, its fundamental purpose is survival. When sex is aligned with love, you have a truly wonderful relationship – as perfect a union between the two universes as is possible.

The next chapter deals with resolving relationship problems that result from differing viewpoints.

CHAPTER 9

Relationship repair

No man is an island entire of itself … never send to know for whom the bell tolls, it tolls for thee. (John Donne, 1624)

John Donne's words can be applied to the whole of civilization. Civilization revolves around relationships; they are the very woof and warp of life, the very fabric of life.

Relationships are the driving force of survival, whether the physical connection between a male and a female in the creation of progeny (survival of the species); the connection between a manager and a staff member; the connection between a player and a team captain, or a player and another member of a team.

No matter how wide and how far you extrapolate the concept of relationships, they are involved in every facet of life. Some relationships are stormy and some placid, but no matter what the connection, one's survival is very dependent upon them. In the case of Charles Dickens' Ebenezer Scrooge, the only relationship this miserly, self-centered individual enjoyed and considered of value was a connection with money. However, in creating wealth and possessing money he nevertheless had to relate to others. He had, for example, a relationship with his clerk, even though he looked upon that downtrodden individual as a possession. Indeed, no man is an island!

On the point of possession, when possession enters into a human relationship it is very much a one-way flow: the possessor has scant regard for the other's feelings and it is invariably an unhappy relationship. In a family situation it results in what is now commonly referred to as 'dysfunction'. In these cases, the 'possession' may be either a spouse or offspring. The domineering father is a classic example of this possessive attitude. A truly happy relationship involves respect for the other or for the other's viewpoints and a free exchange of views.

The writer of the following was a product of an abusive family environment, but a *relationship repair* action completely rehabilitated her life.

In October 2002 I was given back my life. After 12 years of ongoing emotional upheaval through events that ran like a bad soap opera, I had lost my health, my home, my job and people that were precious to me, but most of all I had lost myself. I feel that most of this was created from all the baggage I carried around from an abused childhood. As a family friend once said, 'You kids weren't brought up, you were dragged up.'

By 2002 I was ready to give up, there seemed no reason to carry on this life that had become a confusion of emotional pain, loss and depression. I had forgotten how to laugh or enjoy the wonderful and simple pleasures I had previously known. A dear friend suggested I see John Mace. I'd tried all the usual counseling and anti-depressants with only temporary relief, so I was skeptical, but I went and my life began its turn-around. After a few sessions I was feeling more positive about myself but something still nagged at me. John in his wisdom suggested I carry out a relationship procedure to do with a person (in this case my father) who had had such a negative influence on me. That session was the key. Once those negative beliefs, feelings and emotions were negated I began to live again.

I no longer reacted badly to triggering events; the raw emotions and overwhelming tears just weren't there. It was a joy to wake in the early hours of the morning and revel in the peace I felt and knowing that at last I had been given a tool so simple yet so powerful that I could access in the event I needed it. What a marvelous sense of freedom and empowerment! I have since done several relationship sessions and marvel at the results. I feel like I've been wearing extremely dirty, cracked glasses for so long and have been given a new pair to view life in a positive, healthy way. My thanks seem inadequate

but nevertheless, I thank you.
JD Perth WA

Today, *relationship repair* is a standard action in all cases, so it is appropriate at this point to refer back to the relationship section of the session transcript when the prompt used by the practitioner was, 'Who or what has most adversely affected you?' Although interpersonal relationships are the predominant feature in life – hence the 'who' in the above prompt – it has to be understood that people also relate to groups, organisations and 'things'. It is the client's attitude to them that has to be addressed – hence the impersonal 'what' in the prompt. Answers relating to 'what' have included religion, church, sex and money, to name only a few.

Not withstanding the above, it probably does not require stating, but the relationships, which are of paramount concern in society, are, as John Donne implied, with other people. Examples include a mother relating to her daughter, a business manager relating to his staff, or a husband relating to his wife and children. In the case of a business manager with a staff of 20, it can be said he is relating to the staff as a whole, but 'the whole' is made up of 20 individuals and the real relationship is between the manager and each individual. The most fundamental or simplistic relationship is between two people: there is an interchange of energy between two individuals, so that the basic building block in each and every human relationship is the individual. The success, happiness or love achieved from any relationship is dependent on the individuals concerned, and this in turn depends on the emotional stability and attitudes of each participant as an individual.

It may very well take two to tango, but left unsaid is the assumption that they are both doing the tango – one is not trying to do the waltz! In that situation, the outcome requires no explanation. The first requirement for a fulfilling relationship is a common purpose, a common interest mutually shared. Although a common purpose is necessary in any fruitful relationship, the blossoming or failure of any relationship depends on the attitudes of each individual.

There is more heartache over broken and failed relationships than from probably any other single cause, but just because the common goals and purposes vanish does not mean that the relationship should descend into acrimony, name calling and finger pointing. The optimum outcome when separation takes place is a mutually agreeable parting of the ways and, as Utopian as that may sound, it is definitely achievable once the negative attitudes are out of the way. It is well worth remembering that when someone points their finger at anyone else, there are always three fingers pointing back at themselves, and it is this circumstance that affords the resolution of any relationship that has hit a rocky road. Provided the common goals and purposes are still there and there is a desire to repair the relationship, it is easily achieved. On the other hand, even with the death of common goals and purposes, an amicable parting is certainly achievable.

The divorce courts are full of couples whose attitude towards each other has changed; they married with stars in their eyes, but the twinkle of the stars faded, to be replaced all too often with the flames of anger and animosity. Love, the high aesthetic emotion, has been replaced with mood levels from the other end of the spectrum. There are many apparent reasons for this change, but the inescapable fact is that, rightly or wrongly, they now see each other in a different light.

In any relationship, how one party sees the other is unique. No two people see another in exactly the same way. How a person sees his father is not how his mother sees him as a husband, and it is not how his father's own mother sees him, or his workmates, or his brother or sister. You can expand this concept as wide as you like, but no two people will have exactly the same opinion of another, for, figuratively, they are each wearing tinted glasses that color their view of the other.

No one is all bad, and it is the perceived negative characteristics that cause the problem. But it must be understood that the perceived negative characteristics may not be perceived as such by someone else: what matters is how the viewer sees them and the construction he or she puts on them. This means that, in the language of Causism, each person will have created an image of the other person – an identity of the other – and it is the identity of the other that the person has created to which his or her own negative identities re-act.

As mentioned above, it is the individual who forms the basis of any relationship, and therefore it is the individual's attitudes, demeanor and emotional stability that are central to any relationship succeeding. If the relationship is not succeeding, these factors need addressing.

The procedures developed in Causism are all directed towards individuals, to rid them of negative identities. This is why there is always an improvement in clients' relationships, even though only they and not the others with whom they relate have received help. A particular adaptation of the Mace Energy Method has been developed with the express purpose of addressing relationship problems. It has been named *relationship repair* and features in the transcript in Chapter 7. As simple as this procedure is, its effects are enormous and extend beyond the immediate relationship in ever-widening circles, as the person's changed demeanor rubs off on other associates. Even in isolation, it can and does create miracles, as the following testimonial – from a woman, 60 plus years old – verifies.

> My husband and I were walking on the beach this morning and discussing how lucky we were to be able to live in and enjoy such lovely surroundings, when he added, 'and to find peace at last in ourselves and our relationship'.* This is thanks to you John and your amazing sessions, particularly the relationship sessions. Since then we have no stress, no upsets and our lives and relationship just flow. There is no undercurrent tension – it has been nothing short

184

of miraculous. We have both been on the personal growth path for years, but your wonderful technology has set us both free to just be – any upset is just like a hiccup, there and gone.

Many, many thanks,

Bl

[*The husband had been under medical care for many years because of depression and panic attacks that had put enormous strains on their relationship.*]

The negative non-survival identities that we all have are the root cause of any animosity in a relationship, any dislike of the other. Any intolerance towards the other is because the identity of the other that has been created contains more negative attributes than positive attributes – the other is 'not seen in a good light'. This is where the three fingers pointing back come into play: the owner of the three fingers has his or her own negative identity that is re-acting to the negativity he or she sees in the other.

Identities and relationship problems

The diagram on the next page shows a scenario in which a mother and daughter are having problems with each other. Each is re-acting to the other, but in this instance the problem is being viewed from the mother's viewpoint. She is re-acting to her daughter's apparent shortcomings. The word 'apparent' is appropriate because, like beauty, the shortcomings are in the eyes of the beholder. *Re-act* means to reply or behave in an irrational manner, whereas *respond*

185

means to reply or behave in a rational manner. To re-act always makes things worse, but when a person responds, it is always right for them.

With regard to her daughter, the mother has two identities: the one that she activates in any dealings with her daughter and the one she has created of her daughter. Both have predominantly negative traits, hence the personality clash. Both of these identities are within the mother's own universe. The conflict is really between these two identities, which, of course, manifest by engendering discord.

The same is true of the daughter.

We are not into a blame situation here, because the mother's own identity is just as much responsible for the discord as is the daughter's behavior, irrespective of the nature of the behavior. There is no need to become involved in a lengthy discussion about what caused what, what identity came first, or who is right or wrong. We are faced with a fait accompli and that is that. We have two people, each with a predominantly negative identity of the other, so that each responds in an irrational manner to the other – in other words, re-acts.

RELATIONSHIPS

BEFORE

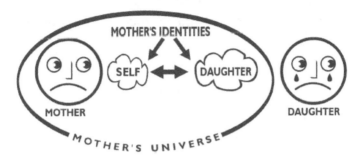

AFTER

Again, it is only the identities in the mother's universe with which we are dealing in this exercise. From a technical point of view, it is therefore the mother's identity that causes the problem, because it is her identity that is re-acting to her daughter's attitude. This may seem a little harsh, but when the mother is able to respond rationally to her daughter's perceived shortcomings, to be more understanding and more objective about them instead of re-acting to them, then and only then will the situation resolve. What particular rational response the mother adopts is not an issue. The operative word is *rational*, and it will depend entirely on the particular situation and circumstances.

Case history

The following is a case history of a mother who is having problems with her daughter, but the same illustration and explanation could apply to any relationship problem.

In this case the mother is attempting to resolve the situation, so the drawing on the previous page and the explanation are from her viewpoint and not that of her daughter. It must also be understood that we are referring to two identities in the mother's universe – they are both the creation of the mother. In the 'before' scenario it can be seen that in the mother's universe there are two identities, each of her own creation. The right-hand identity is how she sees her daughter and the left-hand identity is the one she uses to deal with her daughter – a classic example of cause and effect. Each of the identities in the mother's universe has a predominance of negative characteristics that are causing the friction between them.

The daughter will have a similar pair of identities. Her identities are different in content because they will be in her own universe, and based on her view of her mother. Every identity is a collection of traits. If it is a positive identity, the positive traits predominate, but if it is a negative identity, the negative traits predominate and prevail. Let us construct the mother's two negative identities.

Before proceeding, it should be noted that itemizing the various traits of any negative identities being addressed is no longer necessary, but they are included to give a better understanding of the influence that the various traits have on a relationship.

How she sees her daughter	*Her own identity*
Lazy	Angry
Leaves the bathroom untidy	Bossy
	Antagonistic
Does not make her bed	Cold
Swears	Aloof
Lies	Impatient
Antagonistic	Perfectionist
Disrespectful	Loud
Argumentative	Critical
Bullies her sister	Hates
Cheeky	
Sullen	

It is usually the case that when a person finds a characteristic such as hate in one of their identities, they are a little taken aback to think they were harboring such an emotion. But the emotion is not theirs; it is in their unknowingly created negative identity.

Handling a relationship problem is very simple, as demonstrated in the earlier session transcript, but its simplicity belies its effectiveness. This is not an exercise in changing the daughter. What happens is that with her two negative identities dis-created, the mother can see the daughter through rational eyes. She is no longer viewing her daughter through her own negative identity or, to put it another way, her view of her daughter is no longer clouded by her own negative viewpoint. She is no longer thinking and acting irrationally. From a practical point of view, she has discarded the hypothetical colored glasses labeled 'daughter' and replaced them with a pair of glasses with clear lenses. The mother originally saw her daughter as being lazy; maybe she is, but the mother is no longer viewing her through the eyes of a perfectionist, and has dropped the tendency to be critical. Maybe the daughter was antagonistic because of the mother's continuous criticism, for, as said above, it takes two to tango! The one thing that can be said with certainty is that the mother will *respond* to unwanted behavior on the part of the daughter, but that she will now do so with more tolerance and understanding. If she speaks to her daughter about some unwanted behavior, she will definitely do so in a more constructive manner. If you were to ask her how she now feels about some aspect of her daughter's behavior, she will be noticeably more matter of fact and will probably say something such as, 'That is her problem,' or 'She will learn.' She is no longer unduly and adversely the effect of her daughter.

In the longer term, because the mother has dropped any adverse flows towards her daughter (as in the 'after' drawing in the diagram), the daughter cannot help but develop a different viewpoint of her mother, because the mother has definitely changed, therefore creating a different flow between the two. Optimally, the daughter should have the same handling, but that is a bit Utopian, although in my own practice it has happened a few times.

Further case histories

John Avery, a very successful practitioner with a remarkable ability to relate to children, told me the following story.

One of his clients asked him to help her daughter, who was very unhappy at school, where she felt another girl was very antagonistic towards her. The daughter, who was a primary school student, agreed to be helped, so John used the *relationships repair* handling with her. Shortly afterwards, the mother told John that what happened was beyond her wildest dreams: the two antagonists were now 'best friends'. But there was more to it than that. When John later spoke to the child, she proudly told him that whenever she feels put out by someone she makes herself bigger than the other person, and then she just laughs. Out of the mouths of babes!

A recent case concerned a woman who made an appointment for both herself and her 17-year-old daughter. As they entered my room for a preliminary discussion, the daughter's belligerence and antagonism were palpable. As soon as they were seated, I looked at the daughter and said, 'Are you here because you want to be here or because your mother brought you?' The answer she gave was exactly what her demeanor and body language indicated: 'Because Mum brought me!' 'Okay,' I replied. 'You are not looking for help from me, so I will not attempt to give you any. You can wait in the garden while I talk with your mum.'

With a winning smile on her face she started to get up, but the smile vanished as quickly as it had appeared when her mother turned her wrath on her. She had not driven her daughter 100 miles to see me for nothing! She was going to have some help whether she wished it or not! I interrupted with the obvious question of the young lady, 'Do you want any help?' and I received the obvious answer – she was too antagonistic to be anything but honest – 'No! I want to be left alone!'

It is important to mention that there is no way you can *help* a person who does not want help, nor can you change anyone who does not want to change. The *need to change* is in the eyes of the observer; it is certainly not a wish of the individual under scrutiny. That person is happy the way they are. Even if their behavior could be classed as anti-social, they have no desire to change.

In this particular case I became a mediator between an angry teenager and a mother who was oscillating between grief and anger. Eventually it was agreed that the daughter could go into the garden and the mother would have a session with me, which was, of course, the *relationship repair* procedure.

About 30 minutes later, after a few moments of mutual laughter, we walked together into the garden. The daughter got off the garden bench, a bit apprehensive and not knowing what to expect, but she certainly didn't expect the smile on her mother's face or the arms her mother put around her. Not a word was said, and none was needed, but as they left, the mother turned to give me a hug (the best reward of all) and, having the final word while patting the girl's shoulder, I said to her, 'I do understand.'

There is a major difference in how one approaches a standard session and how one approaches a *relationship repair* session. In the former, you direct a client to an upset that yields the two subtle identities of unknown qualities, or you ask for an unwanted feeling. In the relationship session, it is different. There are, so to speak, two negative identities on a platter. Any discord between two parties must have as its source the two identities in the relationship. This does not mean that you know the details, but you certainly know the mechanics, and that there are two identities to address and dis-create.

It is fair to say that handling a relationship is the most rewarding action a person can take, for, as already noted, the world revolves around relationships. They are the very woof and warp of life. The keys to every troubled relationship are the two identities in each person's make-up. Each person has their own identity and the identity they have created of the other. In each case their *own* identity reacts to the identity they have formed to represent the other, and of course they both sit in their respective universes. *Every disagreement, no matter how many or how frequent, has its source in those two identities.* The magical part is that it is not necessary for both parties to have a session in order to put the relationship on a more rational basis – it is optimal, but not absolutely necessary.

Causism recognizes the difference between *reacting* and *responding* in that the former is irrational and non-survival, whereas the latter is definitely rational and pro-survival – particularly for the person concerned. No matter what the response, it is always right for that person – pro-survival for them. The nature of the response is entirely dependent on the circumstances.

In a broader sense, if party A has a *relationship repair*, their attitude towards part B – their *flows* – changes. Party B notices the change and, in turn, their flows change towards party A. This change continues reciprocating between both parties, so there is a definite change for the better in their environment.

As already mentioned, each party in a relationship has two identities at play, and if it is a troubled relationship, the identities are negative identities. But what is interesting is that as far as Causism is concerned, there is no interest in when, how or why these identities were created.

CHAPTER 10

How to realize your dreams

In the work-a-day world, being successful or making your dreams come true is normally associated with such things as good ideas, hard work, perseverance and even good luck, but we can now add an entirely new element. Before discussing this new element, and whilst recognizing that it cannot be ignored and that it is invariably associated with success, a digression into the more mundane or down-to-earth aspects of being successful will be made. This will provide a more balanced view and a different perspective for achieving success.

Probably everyone knows someone, or at least knows of someone, who always seems to achieve success in all his or her endeavors. Whatever they aim for seems to materialize; sometimes they do not even appear to work very hard to achieve it. A good example is that of people who start a business that just seems to flourish. In contrast, others starting the same type of business may find themselves bankrupt, and may just walk away from their Endeavour to look for employment. They may appear to have worked harder than the *lucky* person did, but it just did not work out for them.

There are, of course, such things as natural business acumen, and that is extremely important, but the words themselves are an over-simplification. Large, prosperous organisations are operating in the field of 'how to be successful', and many books have been written on the subject, so I will only discuss what is probably the basis of so-called business acumen.

Any business, be it a large, international conglomerate or the smallest, one-man show, operates in three basic areas: selling, producing and administration. No matter how many branches and subdivisions are created in large organisations, they all come under the umbrella of one of the above three categories, and they must be financed and operated in that order.

The most important of these areas is selling, followed by production, with administration a poor third. A person is heading for disaster if they invest heavily in administration before they produce anything, never mind having sold anything. The big and showy office with new furniture and equipment is the last thing required to start a business. Production should be limited to sufficient quantities to demonstrate the business's abilities and products. The primary requirement is customers, which incorporates selling.

The great majority of new businesses fail, and they do so because of a failure to follow the natural and fundamental law of selling, producing and administration, in that strict order.

Dick Smith, the Australian businessman, provides a classic example of the application of this natural law. On his web page he almost offhandedly describes how he started his food enterprise. It follows the above criteria to the letter. He was already a wealthy man and could have started out with a grand office complete with all the trimmings, but he did not. He did the opposite, with the bare minimum of expenditure, and even before that he obviously did his research. A second-hand office desk is just as serviceable as a nice new shiny one! It is no stroke of luck that he is a wealthy and successful businessman.

The nature of success

As mentioned in Chapter 2, that great mathematician and scientist Einstein is credited with stating that, as a general rule, people only use 10% of their abilities. Carl Jung went even further in stating that only 1% is used. When viewing humanity at large, this seems to be true, but that *truth* is only an apparent truth. People use all of their abilities, but, unfortunately, the great majority of them are used in the reverse vector – opposing their dreams and aspirations.

Anything a spiritual being decides to do or to have will materialize unless there is overwhelming opposition. On the battlefield, a company of 10 men led by an intrepid and powerful leader will be heading for disaster if they attack a powerful and well-prepared army of 10,000 soldiers. This example demonstrates the equivalent degree of opposition that most mortals experience every day, and explains why there are more people living in poverty than there are wealthy people. The opposition, however, comes from within us. We are our own worst enemies, and this, of course, is the story of negative identities.

Affirmations

The practice of affirmations is a testament to this. The theory behind them and the mechanics of their use form a very important step in understanding the principles and methods of my procedures.

Affirmations are derived from the word affirm, meaning 'to say with certainty and conviction that something is true'. Affirmations are used to counter some negative aspect of life, by autosuggestion. By repeating the positive affirmation, the negative aspect of life is overridden and the positive predominates. When using an affirmation, in the strict sense of the word, people are actually attempting to make the affirmation materialize, and to convince them that what the affirmation says is the truth and what they are experiencing and trying to overcome is a lie. From this it can only be concluded that, deep down, they are intuitively aware that their natural positive outlook is waiting to be resurrected.

Affirmations do not work for everyone – success is variable – and while not seeking to undermine the concept of them, they do provoke some reservations. The success and number of books on the subject demonstrate an underlying truth in the concept. However, many a client has said to me that they have tried affirmations without success. Of course, if they had been successful, they would have had no need to visit me!

For example, in the use of affirmations, if a person is unhappy, they have to keep affirming that they are happy. They are using a positive aspect to overcome a negative aspect. This indicates that something buried in the person's psyche is the unknown source of the unhappiness, and the affirmation is being used to override it. It appears that the first decision a person makes about an aspect of their life becomes the truth. If a person decides, in a moment of utter dejection, 'I will never be happy,' this becomes a truth for them. As sure as the sun will rise in the east, from that moment on, they are never really happy. The Mace Energy Method locates this negative decision and dis-creates it. On viewing the *full* circumstances surrounding the decision, the person, now blessed with hindsight, realizes how negative it is. They realize that it is not true and therefore they erase it. It is important to recognize that with my method the decision is not countermanded with a specific decision such as, 'I will be happy,' or, even more to the point, 'I am happy.'

This is totally unnecessary, for the natural state of all spiritual beings is to be happy. The procedure enables dreams to become reality without the need for the constant use of positive affirmations. The person's natural and inherent happiness surfaces once the negative consideration is erased or dis-created.

This is where the Mace Energy Method departs from affirmations: it locates the source of the negative sentiment and erases it, obviating the need for a positive affirmation to override it. At this point it is appropriate to mention a kindred subject, motivation.

Motivation

As mentioned above, people are naturally happy and optimistic. If they are not, there is something 'foreign' in their make-up that is preventing them from being so. Remove that foreign element and their inherent *joie de vivre* re-surfaces.

Thousands of people attend motivation seminars, looking for that magical piece of information to achieve motivation. Unfortunately, very few achieve their goal. Motivation comes from within, not from without! Some people lose their newfound sense of motivation as soon as they leave the auditorium. For the great majority, it slowly dies as they drift back to their previous way of life with their previous attitudes.

It is ironic that people who attend motivation seminars are looking for something they already possess – namely, motivation. They were *motivated* to go to the seminar! It is ironic that the elusive 'something' they are hoping to find when they go to the seminar is not something they *lack*, but rather something they *have* that is holding them back. That something is a negative consideration locked from view in their psyche – a negative identity. Locate that part of their make-up, that negative identity that is holding them back, free them from it, and the good things will just happen.

The universe of each and every one of us is a complex mixture of positives and negatives – like the positive and negative terminals that enable electricity to be generated and utilized.

It is the existence of the negatives within us that causes so many of our dreams to fail to materialize. When we wish for something, we are saying, 'I would like that,' rather than saying, 'I am going to have that.' A vast difference in attitude is inherent in these two statements. When a person 'wishes' for something, they are really saying, 'I cannot have that but it would be nice if I could.' The 'cannot have that' is coming from an underlying negative decision or consideration that is buried from view in their psyche.

Another concept is relevant here: *real* strength and success come from certainty, but weakness and failure come from uncertainty. Uncertainty is usually followed by *effort*, which is a sure sign that there is a prior negative or counter intention in existence. It goes like this: dream – decision – counter decision triggered – effort

– effort – effort… Once effort has been introduced, the chances of the dream materializing are limited. The natural state of things for a powerful spiritual being is: dream – decision – dream materializing as reality.

The use of 'effort' indicates with absolute certainty that a negative or counter intention is already in place. It is very subtle, but as soon as a person makes a positive decision, any negative decisions that exist are triggered. If any effort to achieve something takes place, the negative decision must have been in place before the positive decision was made. Decisions that are made with absolute certainty will materialize, but the trick is for them to be made with absolute certainty – without a counter decision being introduced or triggered.

Unfortunately, the pessimist, overwhelmed by negative identities, finds it impossible to override them, so that the negatives keep surfacing. The optimist has more positive than negative identities, so negative thoughts do not surface. Pessimism and optimism can be fleeting or permanent states, acute or chronic, and dictate the attitudes and demeanor of individuals.

Fortunately, optimism is an inherently natural state and is easily recovered by using the Mace Energy Method to address areas of negativity.

As affirmations demonstrate, the first decision is the one taking precedence and is, for practical purposes, the *truth*. Positive or pro-survival decisions are normal and natural, so it is only the negative decisions that need locating and dis-creating.

Two personal examples

Some years ago, I applied for a position that I really wanted, so I put a lot of emphasis on my application being successful – I was *efforting*. By this I mean that I was continually thinking about my chances of being successful, waiting for the phone call or the postman. At the same time, I developed a physical complaint that had me really worried and made me pessimistic about my long-term health. The doctor I visited organized a battery of tests, after which, with a smile on his face, he informed me that I had absolutely nothing to worry about in the long term. There was nothing physically wrong.

This doctor, unfortunately now deceased, was a fascinating guy, for after telling me that there was no physical reason for my bodily pains, he told me to lie down on his examination table. He then proceeded to use a kind of 'laying on of the hands', which I now realize is very reminiscent of the Chinese healing art of Gi-Gong and also Reiki, which I have since studied and, in the past, practiced. He focused my attention on various areas of my body by placing his hands there for a few seconds, which resulted in associated negative energy ridges dissipating. (I would love to be able to tell him of my own work in this area.) Very quickly, two things happened. First, there was a gradual lessening of bodily discomfort, and then second – and importantly – I found myself outside my body, enjoying the bliss often accompanied by this state. Then, literally out of nowhere, I was thinking quite calmly and matter-of-factly, 'I am going to get that job.'

Next day, the phone rang and the company director making the call apologized for the delay in responding to me after my interview and offered me the position. This was not a coincidence. I do not believe in coincidences.

Please do not read into this that the practice of Gi-gong or Reiki will end with a person being out of their body – I make no such claim. What happened to me was a combination of various circumstances, and is not the import of what I relate. Additionally, being aware of being exterior to my body is not an unusual circumstance for me. So much for positive decisions!

Years before that happy event, I was going through what can only be described as a personal domestic crisis. I wanted to expand my skills as a counselor, so enrolled in a course to do so, but, among other things, the money and time involved only exacerbated the personal issues. In a moment of utter despair, and in a vain attempt to resolve my personal problems, I gave in and ceased my training. The personal issues did not resolve, so I eventually started a new life. Even so, 2 years later, my desire for more knowledge by way of more training had not materialized. An obstacle always seemed to prevent me: I needed a holiday! I will start after Christmas! There was always a good reason to justify my attitude. I even got around to starting once, but did not continue – for a good *reason*, of course!

Then something remarkable happened. I met

a supervisor from my original course, who, after expressing surprise at my failure to continue, said, 'When you said you had decided not to continue I thought it was only a temporary thing. I did not dream it meant permanently.'

I looked at her in amazement and was then overcome with grief as the circumstances of my ill-fated decision came back to me. They had been occluded and locked away, buried under the emotional pain and turmoil of that period. I recalled saying to a confidant in a moment of utter despair, 'I will not train any more!' That decision had been buried in my psyche, where it had been completely forgotten, but it had been sitting there like a hypnotic command, which I was powerless to overcome. Like all hypnotic commands, I was certainly living it out.

Having exposed the negative decision, I was free of it, and I have never stopped expanding my skills and researching since that moment. But I cannot help but wonder what direction my life would have taken had it not been for that chance meeting. I certainly would not be writing this, but then again, I do not believe in coincidences!

The decision to cease training had been made from despair and apathy, with no thought as to the possibility of circumstances changing. In other words, nothing was even considered to qualify the decision, let alone counter it.

The same applies to being successful in life. While in my doctor friend's rooms, there was not the slightest hint of doubt about me getting the position – negative thoughts were conspicuous by their absence.

These two incidents have told me that there are two circumstances in which decisions will always eventuate: when a person is very down, and when a person is very high. The trouble is that when a person is very down the decisions are always negative, and non-survival, although they are exactly the opposite when the person is very high.

To be realistic about this, it needs to be accepted that the two states mentioned above are generally the exception rather than the rule, but they do serve to explain the mechanics of success or failure in life, and the struggle or ease with which we achieve our goals.

The more negative identities that are removed, the higher the individual's stable mood level and the more often good things just happen. The only thing impeding a person's dreams and aspirations are negative identities. The fewer negatives a person has buried away, the greater the chance of success and happiness in life, and the greater the chance of living his or her dreams.

PART 4

Where It All Began

CHAPTER 11

My story

An astral journey

My life story has two distinct phases, before 1959 and after 1959, and the 'before' and 'after' years are like the proverbial chalk and cheese. That watershed year saw me as an established 32-year-old Master Mariner with 17 years of, shall we say, colorful maritime experience behind me. More than once it has been said to me, 'You should write a book about your life at sea,' but that will never happen, for those years are totally insignificant in the overall picture.

I do not believe in coincidences, so what caused me to be in Fremantle, where my parents and siblings lived, instead of in Sydney, where my own family lived? I had left my ship in Singapore to take some well-earned leave, and instead of flying direct to Sydney, I diverted to my old hometown for a few days, to say hello after an absence of many years.

One evening, my elder brother introduced me to the ideas on time expounded by Count Alfred Korzybski and featured in Chapter 4. To understand what happened, it is necessary to know that as a Master Mariner I was quite proficient in celestial navigation, and that when a ship is in the middle of the Pacific, for instance, you cannot determine its position, no matter what celestial objects are visible, without an accurate time piece – the chronometer. Time was an essential commodity and I knew all about it.

But when confronted with the truth of Korzybski's explanation of time, my world turned upside down. With the sudden reality shift concerning time came another reality shift: not only was I no longer aware of sitting in a lounge chair but, in a flash, I was also no longer a pragmatic Master Mariner with both feet planted firmly on Mother Earth. I was a timeless unit of awareness, alone in the ether. The sense of being alone was absolute, for there was nothing apart from me – no one else, no physical universe, just me, an astral entity, alone in space and surrounded by a great void. There was no sense of night or day, just a vast emptiness, a vast nothingness. The entire physical universe had disappeared! I felt no emotion of any kind; my only feeling was an awareness of myself, of just being there. Then, from what can only be described as light years away, a kind of wispy something began to form, like flimsy clouds drifting around me, and with it came an awareness of utter stillness. I was the focal point, utterly motionless, in the midst of a stillness that no words can describe. That 'wispy something' was the physical universe starting to materialize.

As I write this now, nearly half a century later, the knowledge of that experience is as fresh as if it had occurred this morning. If I choose to close my eyes and relive it, as I have done many times, three facts, afforded by hindsight, stand out in stark relief: the complete absence of time, memory and what is called emotion. Because time did not exist, I have no idea how long the experience lasted. I had no memory of anything, not of family or friends, and it was as if I had never had an earthly existence. I cannot say that I felt serene or calm, as I felt nothing, only an awareness of me, devoid of any sensations.

As the wispy something moved around me, a sense of ennui emerged and, just as suddenly as it had started, the experience ended, leaving me aware of my body again, which was still sitting in a chair in the lounge room.

I have often pondered that experience and tried to find words to describe it. The closest description I could come up with is boredom, or its synonym ennui, but that is woefully inadequate, for the experience was so profound that no single word in the English language suffices to explain the feeling. Several years ago, however, the word came, but it was a coined word, not in any dictionary – *purposelessness*. If you can imagine having absolutely no purpose whatsoever, you will understand what I experienced.

As soon as the sense of purposelessness emerged, the utter futility of just 'being' sent me crashing back to my earthly existence. Having no purpose is the most devastating thing that a being can experience, at least from my perspective.

Until now, that event has been shared with only a very select few outside my immediate family, but after nearly 50 years, and the publication of my research, I guess it's time to bite the bullet and relate the whole story, and the profound effect it had on me.

A new understanding

The immediate effect was of stunned disbelief, mingled with a sense of knowing, but of not being aware of what it was I knew. If asked *what* I knew, the only answer I could have given – with the same certainty that I have felt about it ever since – was that there is no such thing as time and that I had total certainty as to my immortality.

The awareness of being an immortal entity is of incalculable personal significance, but of equal significance on a broader plane was the newfound realization of the nature of time. In addition to this understanding, I had a much more general and non-specific sense of knowing – a knowing feeling. It was as if I knew all the secrets of life.

Many a person has said to me, 'You're a genius John!'

but my response is that I am not a genius. Everybody else knows what I know, but they are unaware that they know it. The only difference between you and me is that I am aware of much of what I know. You and I are both energy units, spiritual beings that are omniscient and omnipotent. While omniscient means 'all knowing', it does not necessarily mean being aware of what you know. That is the difference between us: I was fortunate enough to become aware of certain truths, and with this understanding egotism does not exist, for deep down you know as much as me.

To help understand that concept, when a person is given some new data, a common response may be, 'That is interesting, thank you.' But others given the same data may enthuse over it and say, 'of course, of course! That is so true! It makes so much sense!' What these latter respondents are really saying is, 'I know that! Thank you for reminding me.' This indicates that their awareness of the *newfound* data was only just below the surface. As already stated, everybody knows everything, but whether they are aware of it is another matter.

The new understanding of life expounded in this book has its genus in the out-of-body experience described above. While the experience and the knowledge acquired are at extreme ends of their spectrum, it must be added that it took 20 years of experimentation, research and clinical experience for the final pieces of the jigsaw puzzle of life to fall into place and for the data to surface as knowledge of which I was consciously aware. Before that 20-year period, 25 years were spent examining the work of others before accepting that the answers I was looking for were yet to be disclosed. Interestingly, the answers were already within me, but I was not aware that I had them.

A change of course

To say the experience changed my life is a vast understatement. It opened a vista of life with limitless horizons and brought forward an immediate change of direction. I was not going to return to my secure employment as a shipmaster; I was going to find shore-based employment.

I was only 32 years of age, but already had about 3 years of experience as a shipmaster, so it is fair to say that I had achieved a reasonable degree of material success in my professional life as a mariner. My personal life however was a disaster, mainly because of my prolonged absences from home. Determined to make a new start in shore-based employment, I realized I needed to improve my managerial skills and so I enrolled in an organisation dedicated to personal efficiency. As it turned out, managerial skills proved unnecessary, as within months of returning to Sydney, I was employed by the Sydney Port Authority as a harbor pilot, on the basis of my practical experience, – but that is jumping ahead. Being a harbor pilot and later a harbormaster was enjoyable, especially as both occupations fulfilled my dream of being shore based, but they had no great significance when compared to the achievements of the rest of my life.

Death on a mountain

A friend and I were using a procedure taught at college to relieve the after-effects of trauma. The basis of this approach was quite valid in that it taught that traumatic experiences leave after-effects that can be detrimental to a person's subsequent abilities and effectiveness. Although I have long since discarded that counseling model, it was that experience that set me on my present course in life.

At 12 years old I had nearly electrocuted myself, and that was what my friend and I were addressing. As I delved into my near-fatal electrocution incident, my friend, sitting opposite me, told me to close my eyes and tell him about the incident and to accept whatever came up. After I had told him all I could, he said, 'Go back to the beginning and tell me about it again.' I repeated my introspection a few times and then found myself drifting into a kind of reverie, with the awareness that I was reliving the near-death experience in vivid detail. I was back in it; not talking about it from memory, but actually reliving it, like a kind of revivification.

Once again, I was in my grandmother's little flat and had decided to attempt to repair the malfunctioning electric lamp standing on the table. I turned the switch at the globe socket to the off position and picked up a small screwdriver. You guessed it! The outlet was turned off, but the supply to the lamp was not! Watched by my younger cousin, I began to dismantle the lamp. As soon as I touched the lamp with the screwdriver, my world exploded and everything went black. I was aware of a terrible shaking, my whole body seemed to be vibrating, but there was no pain, and then – miraculously – I had only an awareness of myself as the shuddering ceased. It was as if my body did not exist.

My cousin later said I had screamed, causing her to scream, which brought our grandmother running. I had been unaware of any sound – of my own screams or those of my cousin – and unaware of my surroundings, until I realized I was lying on the floor. I was on my feet in time to see our grandmother burst in from the garden. For how long I had screamed I do not know. During that time, after the vibrating ceased, there I was, all alone, only me, my world a small cocoon of silence with no awareness of my body, as if it did not exist.

Sitting in the chair opposite my friend more than 20 years later in my state of reverie, I started to relive that sensation of not feeling my body, and then, miraculously, I was suddenly transported to another time and place. I was no longer aware of sitting in a chair opposite my friend, or of being in my grandmother's flat; I was on a mountain, cold, exhausted and alone, lying down in the snow, exhorting myself not to give up: 'Keep going! You can get there! But I am tired! I need a little rest! I've hurt my leg, so I'll lie here for a while!' So I continued to lie there. My legs began to relax and their aching ceased, but although feeling better, I continued to lie where I was. Then the lack of pain in my legs became numbness, and the numbness slowly crept over my body like a welcome soporific, until there was no longer any sense of having a body. Once again it was as if my body did not exist. I felt so peaceful, so weightless, so serene, and was finally aware of drifting away from that inert body lying in the snow, ending that life.

Then I became vaguely aware of being with my friend again. I was not in my grandmother's kitchen or on that distant mountain, but I still felt the same serenity and calm as when leaving that other body on the distant mountain so many years ago. The feeling pervaded my whole being as I sat there, and once more I began drifting away from the body on the chair, experiencing no connection with it, just absolute freedom and detachment. I experienced again the calm certainty that I was not a body; I was something simple and immortal. My present troubled family life was just a distant memory; so distant it was irrelevant, and I was free of it. As the sense of freedom pervaded my entire being, I felt as if I was living in another dimension, with a new existence beckoning. Aware of the beckoning new life, I thought, 'this is beautiful. I think I will just drift off and start again.' At that point, my reverie was suddenly interrupted with another thought, 'I cannot go off like this! I cannot do this to the kids!' I had no sooner had that thought than I was fully aware of my body again, fully in communication with it as it sat in the chair. I could again feel the floor under my feet, and the arms of the chair under my resting hands, and on opening my eyes, my friend was sitting opposite me.

In recalling the incident, I am reminded of the story I had read concerning Group Captain 'Tin Legs' Bader, the fighter pilot who had originally been a pilot in the Royal Air Force in the 1930s and who flew with artificial legs during the Second World War. As a result of a terrible flying accident, he was in hospital, where his legs had been amputated – hence his wartime nickname. According to the account of the story, as he was lying in his hospital bed he became aware that the pain had miraculously receded, and at the same time heard loud voices outside his room. Then the voice of a senior nurse cut in: 'be quiet! There is a boy dying in there!' He realized with a shock that she was referring to him, so he promptly decided he was not going to die – and was once more bathed in the agony that had been driving him from his body.

I recognize in his story the same body phenomenon that I had experienced, but with me it was much more than that. It was three experiences rolled into one, joined by an awareness of self, independent of time, location and circumstance. This leads me to conclude that the feeling of gradually disconnecting from the body is what happens in a natural death situation. In my experience on the mountain, I had fallen and was injured, but there was a gradual knowing disconnection from the body. This seems to be the act of the being departing, at bodily death, in an almost leisurely fashion. The electric shock incident was different; it was anything but leisurely. It was sudden, an instantaneous change in reality. This is obviously what happens in an accident, but the common factor, of course, is being detached from one's body.

In the incident as a 12-year-old boy, my body fell over and I regained consciousness lying on the floor. The word *unconscious* is a strange word to use in this circumstance, because it implies not being conscious, not having recall of the event, such as when you are anaesthetized; but that was not the case. Although I was unaware of physical sensations, such as sound, sight and body position, in an extraordinary way I was perfectly aware of me, the being. How I was separated from the lamp I do not recall, but obviously I fell over and that dis-connection saved my life.

At the time, the incident was shrugged off without any analysis of the experience. I guess youngsters take things in their stride. To say the later experience had a profound effect on me is an understatement of immeasurable proportions, but suffice to say it not only changed how I viewed life, but also put me on a completely new course. I now view my life with a calm certainty about my own existence as an immortal being. The later event occurred when I was in my early thirties, and since then I have pursued an intense interest in the spirituality of human beings, not from a religious point of view, but rather from a secular or scientific approach, culminating in the writing of this book.

The common thread in the three incidents was the

sense of not being attached to a body: as a 12-year-old boy in this life in my grandmother's flat; as a grown man in a previous existence dying in the snow on a distant mountain; and drifting away from a troubled period of this life. Several centuries ago, a revelation such as this would have invited a burning at the stake!

Time vanishes

Shortly after the experience described above, I decided to train as a counselor, and I was doing a training exercise when an event occurred that emphasizes the true nature of time as totally subjective. The exercise was designed to train people to have all their attention on the client, and not be distracted by extraneous events. All that was required was that they learned to sit there and do nothing, except keep their attention on the client. I made myself comfortable in a chair and commenced just sitting there, when the trainer tapped me on the shoulder and said, 'You have done enough,' to which I responded, 'But I have just started!' 'You have been there for 90 minutes,' he replied. Ninety minutes of my time had vanished! I say 'my time' because it had not vanished for the others in the classroom! A quick glance at the clock confirmed that truth!

As surprising as that experience may be for some, it is not that unusual, as I have heard several people relate similar experiences when doing Buddhist meditation exercises. One even related 'losing' 3 hours!

In relating my psychic and out-of-body experiences,

I am aware that many people have experiences of a similar nature, including awareness of past lives that they keep to themselves, fearing disbelief and even ridicule. The more I talk with others, the more apparent this fact becomes.

New thinking, teaching and conservatism

Atheists probably epitomize the concept of the denial of the psyche, for they have no belief in another life to follow this one. An atheist can readily tell you about what he did yesterday, what he is doing today and what he hopes to be doing tomorrow. In denying the concept of past and future lives, he is in fact saying there was no yesterday and no tomorrow, only today. This concept of only today, only now, is very true, but not in the context used by atheists, who are in total denial not only of future lives but also of past lives.

The attitude adopted by those who have no belief in past lives or in their own immortality may change when they become aware that we are in reality energy units that are both invisible and indestructible. This puts their awareness of self on a scientific plane rather than a religious plane.

I have shepherded many people into their past lives and have viewed more of my own; however, I do not advocate delving into past-life experiences for the sake of it. My own research and experience indicate that there is absolutely no need to put people into past lives to resolve current emotional difficulties and, indeed, the research has firmly established that the key to the resolution of emotional difficulties lies in this life's upsets. It has been found that all personal difficulties emanate from the experiences of this lifetime and often, but not necessarily so, from the early formative years – from the moment of conception onwards. When helping people resolve a compulsive behavior, such as an addiction, resolution is often found in their teens, when they are struggling with the transition to adulthood, with attendant issues of independence and responsibility. Resorting to drugs, alcohol and tobacco is too often a tragic reaction to the emotional turmoil experienced at this time.

I am fully aware that many will reject outright the new ideas expounded in this book. Rejecting ideas, new or old, is everyone's prerogative, and history is littered with examples of individuals who have been pilloried, ridiculed and even put to death for new, albeit revolutionary, ideas. Two such examples are Socrates and, of course, Jesus Christ.

Socrates' fate is a prime example of the outcome of conservatism protecting entrenched ideas. He lived several hundred years before Christ in the era of the Great Athenian Democracy, and died in 399 BC. During a devastating war with Sparta, his teachings were considered to be a threat to the established order. He was tried and, in what today would be considered a miscarriage of justice, was condemned to die by self poisoning – drinking Hemlock. Today, he is universally recognized as the father of philosophy, an expression that translates to *love of knowledge* or *love of wisdom*.

Probably the most outstanding example in history of someone who challenged conventional teachings is that of the English physician William Harvey. For about 1500 years before Harvey's time, physicians had accepted – apparently without question, for there is no record of any dissent – the theory of the bloodstream expounded by Galen. Galen was recognized as a brilliant physician, but despite his brilliance, he was, as we now all know, wrong about the operation of the bloodstream: he contended that the flow of blood around the body was more akin to the movement of the tides. From the standpoint of today's knowledge, it is not easy to conceive of such a misconception.

Harvey published his treatise on the circulation of the bloodstream in1628 (Harvey, 1986). Its Latin title translates to *An Anatomical Treatise on the Motion of the Heart and Blood in Animals*. It contended that the heart was a pump, which forced the blood to circulate. This new idea was viewed as heresy, yet today Harvey's treatise is considered to be the most important single volume in the history of physiology. Fortunately for the advancement of medicine, he persisted, despite all the opposition. He lived to see his work accepted, but it appears that it was only after his death that his true worth was suitably recognized.

Another person who, like Socrates, completely lost his battle with authoritarian pressure was the Hungarian physician Semmelweis (1818–1865). In his time there was an abnormally high mortality rate from puerperal fever among women giving birth in hospitals. He realized that it was the doctors themselves who were basically responsible for the deaths when he discovered that the fever was a contagious disease transmitted by the doctors as they moved from one examination to the next. The practice in medicine of doctors washing their hands after examining a patient was completely unknown at that time. Semmelweis' solution was to have all the doctors wash their hands in a dilute solution of chloride of lime after each examination of a patient. The incidence of puerperal fever plummeted, along with the mortality rate. Semmelweis had pioneered the use of antiseptics in hospitals, but it was too simple a solution for such a serious problem! He had run headlong into the entrenched ideas extant in medicine.

What happened next was a classic case of 'Do not confuse me with facts; my mind is made up!' The medical fraternity ganged up on him, he was forced out of the hospital, and the use of chloride of lime was discontinued. The mortality rate climbed again and poor Semmelweis ended up in a mental institution, where he died. What is tragically ironic about this is that he died in the same year that the British surgeon Lister pioneered the use of antiseptics in surgery. Semmelweis is remembered today in the form of a statue in the Hall of Immortals in Chicago, USA, and Lister's name lives on with the household antiseptic Listerine, which appears on almost every Australian supermarket shelf, and no doubt in other countries also.

Unfortunately, the experiences of Harvey and Semmelweis are typical of the arch conservatism of the healing profession. With this in mind, it will be interesting to observe the reaction to my findings and procedures!

Underpinning the opposition to new ideas, particularly if they are radical or revolutionary, is the basic human urge of *survival*, as first expounded by that great English philosopher Thomas Hobbes. Opposition to new ideas often stems from a perceived, but usually non-existent threat to the survival of the detractors – in some cases their financial well-being, in others their status, in others their ego. Added to these considerations is the entrenched belief in the validity of what they have been taught. Knowing this allows me to be quite philosophical about the situation, for I cannot change it, but can only emulate the bamboo and bend with the wind, as shown in the following story from my earlier days.

Bending with the wind

As the result of several exhausting days (but more of that later), the old me was in an unusually deep sleep, oblivious to the cares of the work-a-day world. It was a few hours after midnight, in what mariners call the middle watch, when those cares were suddenly thrust upon me with brutally grim reality. The first thought, before being aware of why I was so suddenly awake, was one of personal orientation, 'Where am I?' and then, suddenly fully awake and realizing that I was no longer in dreamland, 'I am on a ship!... I am the master...Oh my god, she's ashore!' It was the shuddering halt of the ship driving ashore at full speed that had catapulted me into sudden wakefulness, to confront the fact that one of a mariner's worst fears had occurred: my ship had run ashore.

It is amazing how one reacts at times. Instead of jumping up out of my bunk, I rolled onto my back, collected my thoughts and lay there for a few seconds, utterly resigned to the fact that there was nothing I could do to change what had happened, and waited for events to unfold. I guess the previous three days had left me with a feeling of resignation to life's vicissitudes.

I did not have to wait long. In quick succession, there came first the loud clanging of the engine-room telegraph, then stillness and calm as the throbbing of the diesel engines ceased, and then the sound of the Second Mate's voice shouting at me 'Wake up Captain. We're ashore!' My immediate thought was 'He must think I am a damn good sleeper!' and then, while stirring myself into action, 'Where in the hell are we? I gradually remembered: 'We're heading for Gorontalo... But there are no islands around here!' And again, 'So where in the hell are we?'

The confusion vanished when my mind dredged up a picture of the chart we were using and the course we had laid the previous evening. That course had us safely passing a headland on our starboard side in the early hours. 'My god, we have hit the bloody headland! How did we get in there?' As it turned out, the lighthouse on the headland was out! The ship had set to the east! The second mate claimed he had mistaken the very steep and high coastline for rain clouds, but that was later. For now there was the clang of the engine-room telegraph above my head, the second mate's shout, 'Captain! Wake up! We are ashore!' and my reaction 'He must think I am a damn good sleeper!'

Up on the bridge the stark truth was thrust home. The ghostly glow of phosphorus in the waves that broke in the shallows on either side of the ship was the only sign of movement.

After what seemed an interminable delay, a sigh of relief greeted the information that internal soundings showed the ship was dry – in other words, we had not been holed. The waves were not big enough to cause concern, so we were not in any immediate danger. We had a hundred or so passengers on board and, as daylight broke, the boats were lowered and the passengers were taken ashore to a nearby village. With all of them ashore, I was able to concentrate on saving the ship, not to mention my reputation!

Daylight revealed why we were not holed. We were sitting on sand, but only a stone's throw away on either side was the rocky shoreline – going ashore there would have left any hope of salvage out of the question. It was almost too good to believe, but we were stranded on the only sandy patch to be seen.

The beach was very steeply shelved where the ship went ashore. The bow was almost out of the water, but there was about 100 feet of water below the stern.

Although the seas were comparatively small, the ship was enduring crippling stresses, as evidenced by the internal creaking as the stern section moved to the gentle swell while the fore part was stuck fast. The nearest salvage tug was in Singapore, which was many days' steaming away, provided of course it was not attending some other unfortunate mariner.

One look at the inhospitable coastline made me determined that I was not going to be left ashore there, as the likelihood of the ship quickly becoming a total loss was very real. The nearby village did not offer much cheer either.

Calculations indicated that without outside help our only hope was to lighten the ship's load, particularly at the forward end. We had a large supply of water to cater for all the passengers and this was quickly pumped overboard, and some fuel transferred further aft. Along with the dumping of water, the major benefit would be gained by also dumping cargo from the two forward holds. There was a large consignment of bagged sugar there, and all hands, augmented by some labor from the nearby village, were set to jettisoning it.

Later that day, an Indonesian army major appeared from nowhere. Apparently the sugar I was dumping was government property. He laid a .45 caliber revolver on the table and made it clear that no government cargo was to be jettisoned! Despite protestations and explanations about insurance, he was adamant that if the ship could only be saved by dumping government property, well it could stay where it was! You can draw your own conclusions as to what he had in the back of his mind, but the revolver deterred further conversation, leaving me frustrated, inwardly fuming, and wondering what was going to go wrong next.

I can laugh about it now, but nearly 50 years ago it was no laughing matter. I had no belief in prayer and decided that even if there was a God, he only helped those who helped themselves. So, not to be beaten, I had the lifeboats stripped of fittings and turned them into barges, using awning spars from the upper deck to form a platform between pairs of boats. It was not a brilliant innovative idea on my part: I had recalled reading about such an exercise during my maritime studies, although at that time my thoughts were, 'what a lot of rubbish! Who would have to resort to that in this time and age!' How wrong can you be!

To continue the story,[2] when loaded, the improvised barges were towed by our launch to a nearby beach, which was around a little headland about 20 minutes' travel away – the landing point being the village where the passengers had sought shelter before making their way to Gorontalo. This is where the sugar was landed, albeit somewhat soaked and ruined by salt from being carried through the shallows. The process was frustratingly slow compared with jettisoning.

---

2   Should any experienced mariner read this, please understand that I have glossed over the more technical aspects that have no particular bearing on the thrust of the narrative.

On the second day, the captain of a passing ship, hoping to earn some salvage money, vainly tried towing us off at the noon high tide. His departure left us firmly ashore and on our own.

On the third day, the launch that was towing the lifeboats loaded with sugar did not return for several hours. I was almost frothing with rage at the delay. When it did return, the crew was greeted with a blast of anger fed by frustration, for a small headland blocked my view of the beach and I had no idea of what was happening. 'Where the hell have you been?' was replied to with, 'Sorry Captain, but the launch broke down!' Some more bad luck!

I was too busy with the problems to take much notice of the presence of an elderly sightseer who had returned with the crew. I was furious at the delay because I had decided to attempt to re-float the ship at high tide that night and I needed the boats to transport two anchors out behind the ship with wire hawsers attached. The idea was to haul on the hawsers to assist the engines. Laying the anchors was a very slow process, but we achieved it by nightfall.

Midnight arrived and, much to my surprise, for I was making the attempt more in hope than expectation, the ship re-floated. Just days previously, another vessel had been unable to haul us off, yet here we were safely afloat by our own efforts!

On arrival in Gorontalo the next morning, we still had the sightseer aboard. 'Who is he?' I asked of the purser. 'Why is he still aboard?'

'He is the Magic Man. It was him who got the ship off last night!'

I looked at him. I was feeling quite proud of my efforts to save the ship, even if we had lost a lot of cargo, but most of all I felt totally exhausted and I simply boiled over. 'He got the ship off!' I exploded.

'Well I suppose you did,' the purser said, trying to mollify me. 'But he broke the evil spell over us.'

'Evil spell! What the hell are you talking about?'

'It had been over us ever since we sailed from Surabaya.'

I looked at him in stunned disbelief. The total irrationality of his belief left me speechless, and I just turned away with the realization that the launch breaking down had had something to do with the shaman. Indeed, I was later told that the launch had not broken down, but had been used to get the shaman from a village down the coast. The Malaysian deck crew had decided among themselves, with the connivance of the charter's representative, that the only way to save the ship and undo the bad luck that was plaguing the voyage was to recruit the aid of this local shaman.

In my cabin, with a whisky or two to settle me down, my attention went back to Surabaya, where the voyage had started. It was sailing day. The ship, with a Singaporean Malay deck crew, was on charter to a company in Indonesia and we were in Surabaya loading cargo and taking on board passengers for

Sulawesi (the Celebes), with our final destination the port of Gorontalo, in the extreme northeast of the island. We were also scheduled for a stopover of a few days at a small port or anchorage, whose name I have forgotten, about 24 hours' steaming time away from our final destination.

On sailing day, at about 9 in the morning, the local head of the charter company had come into my cabin.

'Good morning captain.'

'Good morning Mr. Tan.'

After a few formalities, I said, 'We will be ready to sail by noon, so you can confirm that with the harbor master and order a pilot.'

'Well, you see, I need to discuss this with you.'

'Is there any problem with a pilot for that time?'

'N.o.o, but we have a problem with sailing today.'

'What is the problem?'

'Well, to be truthful, today is not a good day to sail. It has very bad omens.'

'You have got to be joking! The ship is ready to sail! The passengers are coming aboard now!'

'I know, but...'

The man's voice trailed off when he saw the look of derision on my face. The economics of holding the ship in port because of some local superstition were beyond my reality, added to which I wanted to be on the move. We duly sailed at noon.

At the stopover port there was an epidemic of Asian flu, which I contracted. For three days I was as sick as I have ever been before or since, and although it sounds melodramatic, I was resigned to dying.

For me to be so ill needs putting in perspective. Being ill is not an everyday experience for me, and I have never been prone to sickness. I have no recollection of ever having a single day off from work because of illness. A couple of injuries in my sea-going career had kept me away from work, but I did not have illnesses.

We were there for three or four days, and by sailing day, after some dubious treatment offered to me, I was able to get to my feet and take the ship to sea. After checking the courses for the final leg to Gorontalo, and with the usual instructions to call me if at all in doubt, I collapsed on my bunk. With a good night's sleep, I would be ready for the morning arrival at Gorontalo. But of course it was a few more mornings before that happened.

In Gorontalo, with all that behind me, I was in my cabin getting mellow with whisky and smiling to myself at the ignorance of some people, who honestly believed that a magic man could actually influence day-to-day events. As for getting a ship off the beach, God help me!

A reflection

At the time, it was amusement, not tolerance and understanding, which caused me to 'let sleeping dogs lie'. But today I am pleased that I kept my belittling thoughts concerning their 'naivety' to myself, for although it may sound trite and condescending, it would have been a gross invalidation of the crew and their beliefs. They were doing what they thought was the best way to help, which was kept from me for obvious reasons after the events on sailing day in Surabaya. Their assessment of me was of course correct, for it has to be admitted that any suggestion, no matter how polite, of getting a shaman to help would have been vetoed out of hand.

One can become involved in an endless discussion concerning psychic phenomena in their various guises to explain how the ship got off the shore, and to what extent, if any, my efforts contributed to that happy event. But I will leave the passing of judgment on that score to others. Reflecting on the episode, my feelings are mixed. Given my time again, instead of the classic negative reaction, my response to the company official in Surabaya would be, 'I understand. What about sailing first thing in the morning?' One thing I am sure about is that even to contemplate any psychic help would have been totally foreign to the old me.

Yes, I have changed! I have long since ceased to scoff at anything out of the ordinary, no matter what, as this recent conversation with my wife illustrates.

During morning tea she said, 'the spirit of that young girl seems to have gone. She has not been in the garden for ages.'

'The fact that you thought about her may indicate she is still around.'

'No… I do not feel it is that. As a matter of fact, I have just realized that she has not been around since Bronwyn went to England. Maybe it was only Bronwyn she was interested in, and not us, or our garden.'

'It was certainly not me she was interested in … I have never been aware of her, as I was with Mum for instance.'

'Your Mum's spirit went as soon as you acknowledged her presence, didn't it?'

'Yes. Maybe that is what happened to the young girl's spirit.'

'Could be … I will mention it to you if she should come back.'

I have indeed changed! Gone is the pragmatic, materialistic individual quick to scoff at anything metaphysical: 'Reincarnation! Give me a break!' 'Ghosts! Show me one and I will believe you!'

Yes, I have indeed changed.

APPENDIX 1

References

Barker, Joel Arthur (1993). *PARADIGMS. The Business of Discovering the Future.* HarperCollins, New York.

Bernstein, Morey (1956). *The Search for Bridey Murphy.* Doubleday & Co., Garden City, New York.

Dresden James Quotes. Google Internet Search, 2005

Harvey, William (1986). *The World Book Encyclopedia.* World Book Inc., Chicago.

Hobbes, Thomas (1991). *Leviathan.* Cambridge University Press, Cambridge.

Johnson, Griffiths (illus.) (1998). 'Your ID please.' *The West Australian.* West Australian Newspapers Ltd, Perth.

Kipling, Rudyard (1972). *Sixty Poems,* seventh printing. Hodder & Stoughton. London.

Korzybski, Count Alfred (1933). Matter, space and time. *Science and Sanity.* The International Non-Aristotelian Library Publishing Co., Lakeville, Connecticut.

Lionni, Paolo & Klass, Lance J. (1980). *The Leipzig Connection.* Heron Books, Portland, Oregon.

Mace, John (2000). *How to Turn Upsets into Energy.* Brolga Publishing, Melbourne.

Nikhilananda, V. (ed.) (1987). *Inspired Talks of Swami Vivekananda (1893).* Ramakrishna Vivekananda Center, New York.

Spencer, Herbert (1937). Ultimate scientific ideas. *First Principles,* 6th edn. Watts & Co., London.

The American Heritage Dictionary (1981). Houghton Mifflin Co., Boston.

The Australian Oxford Dictionary (1999). Oxford University Press, Melbourne.

The World Book Dictionary (1973). Thorndike-Barnhart, Chicago.

Weatherhead, Leslie D. (1935). *Psychology and Life.* Hodder & Stoughton, London.

APPENDIX 2

Testimonials

Practitioners

I am writing to tell you of my experience as a Mace Energy Method practitioner.

It has been so rewarding seeing and hearing the changes in the lives of my clients using the method. These changes have been dramatic and instant with both men and women. The changes include loss of depression, better understanding with family and friends, improved energy levels, better sleep, loss of anxiety plus relief from compulsive and addictive behavior.

I could go on and on. As one client put it, 'Life is so easy now, it is as though a ton of bricks has been taken off my back – I feel so happy, so light and good things just keep on happening.'

I am so glad I had the opportunity to train and become a practitioner – what a gift to me and the world, and it's all so easy.

Thanks once again,

Barbara Louise (*Practitioner*)

****

My journey in this field began in 1963. I had a fairly successful business but I seemed limited – I could not progress past a certain point. Working hard was no problem as it was enjoyable. I was vaguely aware I was holding myself back somehow but I had no idea how.

I commenced searching for the answers as to why some people could set goals and then achieve them with consummate ease, while others, not lacking in effort, could not do so.

This search took me to my first counseling sessions, which certainly made me feel better – a lot of my negativity and self-destructive habits abated. My attitude improved and a very important thing came out of the counseling – I realized I was fully responsible for the results in my life, good or bad, and I stopped blaming others for my problems.

From this improvement I decided that I would like to help others as I had been helped, so in early 1964 I commenced training as a counselor/consultant in Perth. In 1966 I went to England and then Canada and America for more training and experience, which continued into the '80s.

Along the way, despite different methods of healing and motivation, I still felt something was missing. For both clients and myself I noticed that some problem areas would go away, only to resurface again later. It seemed impossible to achieve a permanent change no matter what the skill of the counselor and the good intentions of each party. Something was still missing.

Because I could not achieve permanent results for my clients I felt a little like a fraud, so ceased my counseling activities. My journey so far had led me to realize that many others were looking for the same thing – a permanent solution to overcome the seemingly invisible hurdles in life, blocking happiness and achievement.

For me life has three main areas: work, home and social. There are many examples of one person being great at work but with lots of family and relationship problems, while others are fine socially but can't handle work. Their potential has only been realized in one area. To me, true happiness lies in being on top in all areas.

Today there are many methods of healing or motivation, which can and do make people feel a lot better; that is easy, but how long it lasts is the real criterion. Although not a criticism, for I am full of admiration for those who genuinely want to work with and help their fellow man, I call these *feel good therapies.*

Over the years, because no permanent solution has emerged to handle life's problems, a large part of society has been conditioned to the quick fix, hence the prevalence of drugs, illegal or otherwise. It is as if many people are grasping for any little bit of transient happiness regardless of the consequences.

In 1995 I was in Perth and met up again with John Mace. Our paths had crossed a few times over the years and we had remained friendly because of our similar interests in self-improvement techniques.

John was very excited about a new procedure to handle upsetting experiences, so he took me into his office and demonstrated the technique on a few of my past upsets, although what he used then was quite crude when compared to the exactness of today's procedures.

The full impact of the processing was not appreciated until I arrived home on the East Coast where I had a business. Quite suddenly people started calling for my services, which was puzzling, as I had not been promoting. I asked several why they had called me and one said I had been recommended four months previously. I remained wondering why they had all called on my first week back and then it hit me – the clients had not changed but I had! My flows had opened up, things that had seemed hard before were now easy, and life was much more enjoyable. It was my unseen resistance to success that had evaporated – the negative identities as explained in this book, which had been holding me back, had gone.

It had taken me from 1963 until 1995 to find what had been holding me back – at last the missing part had been found. About a year ago a client came to me with the same problem that I had been struggling with for so many years. In an hour or so his problem area was handled and now his business is booming. John claims that his research has ushered in a major paradigm shift in handling life's viruses. I fully agree.

We are all Spiritual Beings of infinite potential and this is a very important basic truth. Negative identities are the missing link between *just feeling good* and a permanent desirable change to a happy life. I call these identities Spiritual Traps. Instead of us getting what we want in life, these traps give us what we do *not* want.

For me, this technology is very simple but extremely powerful. It is stress free and non-confronting for the client. Eliminating life's invisible barriers can now be achieved by anyone who is genuinely desirous of doing so.

The biblical saying 'Seek the truth and the truth will set you free' is very appropriate when explaining the method. It helps a person find the truth about themselves, to set them free of their unknowingly created negative identities, which oppose their own dreams or goals.

When someone has a dream or goal for the future it is like a forward thrust of energy (motivation), but an upset may cause him or her to decide, for instance, 'I will never be happy!' This opposes their dream of 'a happy contented life'. Imagine your right fist as your dream and your left fist as the identity, then push them against each other to demonstrate the energy used. Surely this helps explain the debilitating Chronic Fatigue Syndrome so prevalent in today's society.

After 40 years of searching, I know I cannot emotionally heal anyone, but I can certainly guide them whilst they do their own healing.

My purpose, created in 1963, 'to help people be happy' is now a reality and achieved on a daily basis. Thanks to John – I *am living my dream! – I am in control of my life!*

Anyone who has a similar dream can achieve it. Professional training is achieved in days and weeks, not months and years.

I feel privileged to have shared this trip with John since 1995.

John Avery (*Mace Energy Method Practitioner and Trainer, Queensland*)

Gambling

I am writing to you to share with you the results of our sessions so far.

Firstly I am relieved of a more recent addiction, that of gambling. This problem caused so many other stresses and upsets in my life and I could never understand why I continued to do the very thing that was causing so much financial hardship, guilt and grief. After only one session, that problem has disappeared. Or should I say dis-created.

Over the last month so much of my life has improved enormously, I am happier, healthier and enjoying all my relationships more and even seeing people through different eyes. I realized the other day that I am even sleeping really well now and have more energy to perform my tasks during the day and I wake up with a great attitude. This technology is amazing, I am so glad that you made it available to me.

With love,

AM

Depression

I am writing to let you know how the session you gave me has improved my life.

In the past fourteen years I have suffered from stress, anxiety and panic attacks. These conditions have affected my life in many different ways. It affected my relationships with my children, my stepchildren and my wife. It also affected my social relationships, my work relationships, and it diminished my chances of gaining meaningful employment, with the result that I was mainly unemployed for the greater part of the last fourteen years.

During that period I sought help from doctors, psychologists, psychiatrists, counselors, groups, medication and also 7 weeks in a clinic. This seeking of help came at a great financial burden to my wife and myself.

I hope this letter in some way explains how my life

has changed and how grateful I feel towards you for helping me.

At last no more panic attacks. No more anxiety.

Reginald

****

Thank you so much for applying your love and skill to my situation. I feel more stable now than I have done in many, many years and I have not had one iota of upset or anger or depression or loss or abandonment since leaving you last Sunday week. Compared with my state of the preceding two and a half months and the many months before, that is truly remarkable.

An enormously big THANK YOU.

SD

****

E-mails from a client resident in Chicago

12th April 2001
Hello,
I'm in such a low mentally depressed state I don't even know how to ask for your help. But can you help me? If you like I will write and tell you my situation... Simply ... I'm a 50 year old woman... who has been unhappy off and on most of my life, for various reasons. I have been told I am manic-depressive. I was on Prozac for 10 years, now I take Effexor and Welbutrin for the last 3 years. If my life seems to be going smoothly without 'issues' to deal with I'm OK. The 'issues' that I can't seem to deal with are personal relationship related.

So now what do I do?

19th April 2001

I am feeling mellow. I see my life a little clearer and sense that I am more grounded. But I'm still in the disbelief stage. How can something so simple be so very effective?

21st April, after another session

I seem to grow more thankful each day for 'assisting me to be my real self.' Thank you from the bottom of my heart...

26th April, after a third session

I feel fortunate to have had this experience with you. This definitely has affected my life like nothing else has ever done.

Thank you for your guidance.

****

Excerpts from a letter by a medical doctor who had been pensioned off due to deep chronic depression

I am a graduate of the University of Queensland, MBBS (1981) and received my FRACGP in 1989... In 1995 a period of serious health problems kept me off work for 6 months and then in 1997 a number of significant stressful events occurred and I developed a major depression for which I received psychiatric care, including medication, insight-oriented psychotherapy, CBT and support from my GP, family and friends.

After four hospitalizations over four years, I was medically retired from my work in March 2000.

This of course was tremendously stressful for me and my recovery has been slow. When my mood lowered again in December 2000, my father (who has known you for many years) insisted I ring you John. He was delighted to learn that you could work with me via the phone.

Having worked with patients and now with myself in the area of mental health for some time, I consider myself very psychologically sophisticated and am pretty perceptive and aware of processes either as they occur or are explained to me. It is from this viewpoint that I talk about my experiences with you. I uncovered the painful nitty-gritty of the 'depression', 'I am no good', 'I'm not worth it', 'I'm unlovable', 'I eat under stress', identities that were triggered under stress and which *I could not control.* As you rightly pointed out, 'what you resist persists', so the identity created leaves a no-win situation – unpleasant negative effects that got worse when I tried to 'fight them off'. Thanks to working with you – *they are gone.* I will not recreate them.

Anyway, I feel wonderful and the times I have felt this way can only be counted in hours to a few weeks over the last 4 years. I am so very grateful to you. I went to a medical meeting last night and it was the best, most relaxed I have ever felt at one. I only started going back to them a couple of weeks after I started with you. I have now attended four, one a weekend one, but none in the prior 12 months. It's very exciting looking forward to getting my life back!

With immense gratitude.

SN

[**Note.** *This lady has now resumed her medical practice.*]

****

From a woman who had been on anti-depressant drugs for 6 years: she had experienced the trauma of the loss of a child and of her husband in tragic circumstances; she is now free from medication

I feel like a new person – confident about whom I am now. The depression has lifted and I feel as though I can handle anything that's put in front of me. I'm a lot happier about life and living.
LC

Postnatal depression

I wish to express my gratitude for the change in my health and well-being since my session with you in early July. To give you a little background, I had suffered with post-natal depression since my first child was born seven years ago. After my second child was born two and a half years later I was experiencing severe exhaustion, panic attacks and anxiety. I was so bad that I was unable to cope with looking after the children and traveled from Melbourne to Perth for help from family for a month to try and pull myself together. The depression, anxiety and panic attacks continued on and off for the next four years. I have tried everything from psychology, acupuncture, kinesiology and hypnotism to ease my anxiety.

After my session with you I felt more confident and calm within. A lot of my anxiety was removed and I feel I can cope with any stressful situation over which I would previously have panicked. I also notice that my physical health and well-being have improved a great deal.

Thank you John.

Sincerely

JS

General

When I was introduced to John Mace I was about 30 years into a lifelong search for self-improvement. Throughout that period I had tried most things at some time or other and, I must say, enjoyed great benefit from some of these.

Given this experience it doesn't take long to spot a fake. And I must confess that the offer of processing or therapy by telephone – London to Australia – sounded a bit implausible given the background I had come from. I was prepared for this not to work. But I was consumed by problems. In spite of a lifetime of search for answers to personal difficulties – and having found many answers en-route – things were simply not going right for me. But if I entertained doubts they were dispelled within about ten minutes.

I knew I had discovered something extremely valuable.

Not surprising, then, that the therapy itself is dead simple. Not to mention fast. The simplest, least complicated, most straightforward 'chatting' with John has changed my life beyond all recognition. And it is not simply about the way I 'feel' but what has happened.

I was verging on being homeless. My marriage was on the rocks. I was flat broke, jobless, working every hour of every day and getting absolutely nowhere. A month later I have a beautiful new home, a wonderful relationship with my wife, a new contract that more than pays the bills and a business that now looks as though it will work.

This is not my imagination. This is real. Oh, and I feel good, too!

There have been a number of clear watersheds in my life. The latest was meeting John Mace. This man is up there with the very best of the best and deserves to be recognized as such.

John is a genius and I am proud to call him a great friend.

GC, *London*

******

In September 1997 I went to Perth Australia to see John Mace for treatment/processing. Over the years I had done many courses in the Human Potential field including processing in USA and Germany. Some of the work was simply ineffective. Some had a short-term effect but it did not last and my basic problems stayed the same.

John and I did a lot of Identity and Upset handling to address various problem areas: a craving for alcohol, low self-esteem, problems in my social environment, career problems, relationship problems with my spouse and even a sexual hang-up. I noticed wins immediately, but was still suspicious as to whether this would last. *It did!*

In the last 7 years I have never had a setback in the areas addressed by John's processing and generally enjoy a high mood level. I can honestly say that John's tech works and guarantees a permanent solution to problems.

TM

[**Note**. *He came to me early in my research and the upset handling referred to is no longer used. It has been superseded by more rapid procedures.*]

****

Thanks for the wonderful 'cut and polish' and your silky smooth handling … I do feel very different and stable. Time will give me more concrete examples of this amazing new state I find myself operating in. It was a joy to see you at first hand practicing your craft.

You have developed and perfected the most

powerful yet simple technology to handle emotional problems on this planet and so take your rightful place along side the great humanitarians of the ages.

I am very proud to have been privileged to have met you and become one of your friends and confidants.

AD (*an engineer*)

****

This processing has helped me to understand how I have dis-empowered myself and how my thoughts create my reality. Not only have I understood it, but also I have experienced it. Now I feel peaceful and able to create my dreams again – for a while I had lost the confidence to dream.

Anonymous

I wish to thank you for the wonderful changes in my life since having that session with you. Over my life I have suffered with depression and anxiety. I've tried many modalities to heal and change this condition that has plagued me: counseling, regression, group therapy, attitudinal healing, breath work, body work, psychologist, John Bradshaw family therapy and co-dependence. They all helped to some degree.

But the depression still reared its ugly head. After one session with you the change is so profound that I have decided to train with you and become a practitioner, as your method is the only modality that has completely eradicated my depression.

Thank you with all my heart.

BM

[**Note**. *As good as her word, this lady is now fully trained.*]

Spiritual awareness

An e-mail to a friend with a copy to me

I have just returned from having some magnificently spiritual counseling from John Mace in Perth, which has got me looking at life, and the way that I interact with it, in the way that I wish to. So I am feeling better than I have done for many years and more than that! I am more centered and loving than I have been at any time this lifetime. Yet more compassion. Yet more love. Yet more sense of service. Yet more strength. Yet more sense of fun, with integrity. Yet more certainty that heaven is within, and connected to all. Bashar's definition of integrity, 'a conscious awareness that one is an integral part of the whole', is for me the most apt English language definition I have come across to date.

Addictions

Thank you for helping me heal my addictions that have caused me so much anguish for almost 15 years.

The amazing thing is that I now have *no* cravings. When you helped me to quit my smoking I was very skeptical that I could ever truly *not want* them, but that's exactly what happened! Today I don't want them any more – and there is no struggle involved. I can also watch others smoke without feeling jealous or any other negative sensation.

My finances, health, self-esteem and general happiness have all improved greatly and will continue to do so. I lead a more positive and productive life now – something I have wanted for so long.

Your unique method of treatment has worked so rapidly for me and I am and will remain deeply grateful.

Thank you for helping me be more of myself.

Love always,

Lisa

[**Note.** *Lisa's addictions had been marijuana and tobacco.*]

Appendix 3

Training and personal help

For personal help and training, John Mace can be contacted via the Internet.

E-mail: macemethod@iinet.net.au

Website: www.macemethod.com.au

The website lists some of the practitioners.

Although the exact procedures are not published separately, they can be found in the session transcript. But experience has demonstrated that, as simple as they are, the best results will only be obtained by someone with formal training. Training usually takes about 3 months rather than years, and is available both in the academy and by correspondence. All the original practitioners outside Australia were trained by correspondence from the Perth Academy.

As explained in the book, it is impossible to use the procedures as a 'self-help' tool – not even the researcher can do that. Therefore, although a greater understanding of life will be achieved from reading this book, it does not fall into the 'self-help' category. However, the technique can be used to some effect with a friend or someone else who has read and understood the information contained within the book, which is why a session transcript has been included.

In the field of research and development, Joel Arthur Barker (Barker, 1993) uses the analogy of explorers, pioneers and settlers. He likens the researcher with new ideas to the explorer who enters the unknown. When he returns unscathed, the first pioneer re-traces the explorer's steps. When he again emerges unscathed, other pioneers, trusting the reports, emulate him, and the band of pioneers grows in number. Increasing numbers of positive reports encourage settlers to open up the new territory. In the case of my own 'exploration', John Avery was the first pioneer, and richly deserves recognition as such. The other pioneers are those who put their trust in me, not only as clientele, but also, very importantly, as trainees. With the help of all the pioneers, this book will usher in the settlers.

The original training academy is still operating in Perth, Western Australia, but other academies and clinics have been established.   Trainers are listed among the practitioners on the web site. Even if there is not an academy within reasonable distance, a major feature of the Mace Energy Method is that it is equally as effective over the phone or Skype as it is in person. The tyranny of distance belongs to yesteryear.

BUY A SHARE OF THE FUTURE IN YOUR COMMUNITY

These certificates make great holiday, graduation and birthday gifts that can be personalized with the recipient's name. The cost of one S.H.A.R.E. or one square foot is $54.17. The personalized certificate is suitable for framing and will state the number of shares purchased and the amount of each share, as well as the recipient's name. The home that you participate in "building" will last for many years and will continue to grow in value.

Here is a sample SHARE certificate:

HABITAT FOR HUMANITY

THIS CERTIFIES THAT

YOUR NAME HERE

HAS INVESTED IN A HOME FOR A DESERVING FAMILY

1985-2005

TWENTY YEARS OF BUILDING FUTURES IN OUR
COMMUNITY ONE HOME AT A TIME

1240 SQUARE FOOT HOUSE @ $65,000 = $54.17 PER SQUARE FOOT
This certificate represents a tax deductible donation. It has no cash value.

YES, I WOULD LIKE TO HELP!

I support the work that Habitat for Humanity does and I want to be part of the excitement! As a donor, I will receive periodic updates on your construction activities but, more importantly, I know my gift will help a family in our community realize the dream of homeownership. **I would like to SHARE in your efforts against substandard housing in my community!** *(Please print below)*

PLEASE SEND ME _____ SHARES at $54.17 EACH = $ $_____

In Honor Of: _____

Occasion: (Circle One)   HOLIDAY   BIRTHDAY   ANNIVERSARY

      OTHER: _____

Address of Recipient: _____

Gift From: _____ *Donor Address:* _____

Donor Email: _____

I AM ENCLOSING A CHECK FOR $ $_____ PAYABLE TO HABITAT FOR HUMANITY OR PLEASE CHARGE MY VISA OR MASTERCARD *(CIRCLE ONE)*

Card Number _____ Expiration Date: _____

Name as it appears on Credit Card _____ Charge Amount $ _____

Signature _____

Billing Address _____

Telephone # Day _____ Eve _____

PLEASE NOTE: Your contribution is tax-deductible to the fullest extent allowed by law.
Habitat for Humanity • P.O. Box 1443 • Newport News, VA 23601 • 757-596-5553
www.HelpHabitatforHumanity.org